ISLAM IN HISTORY AND SOCIETY

ISLAM IN HISTORY AND SOCIETY

MALEK BENNABI

Translated From French and annotated by
ASMA RASHID

KITAB BHAVAN
NEW DELHI-110 002. [INDIA]

ISLAM IN HISTORY AND SOCIETY

KITAB BHAVAN
Publishers, Distributors, Exporters & Importers
1784, Kalan Mahal, Darya Ganj,
New Delhi - 1100 02 (India)

Phone : (91-11) 23277392, 23274686,
: (91-11) 23263383
Mob : +91-9953098606

Website : www.kitabbhavan.net
Email : info@kitabbhavan.net
nasri@vsnl.com

First Published in India 1999
Reprint 2022

ISBN - 10 : 81-7151-279-8
ISBN - 13 : 978-81-7151-279-9

Book Code No. : 100026

Batch ID : SPRFNS130722

Printed & Published in India by :
Moonis Ali Nasri for Kitab Bhavan
1784, Kalan Mahal, Darya Ganj,
New Delhi - 1100 02 [India]

TO MY MOTHER

CONTENTS

[illegible]

FOREWORD

Malek Bennabi (1903-73) could easily be regarded as the most eminent and profound scholar and thinker of post-World War II Algeria, and certainly in his perioc one of the foremost intellectuals of the Arab world. As a philosopher, he could be placed on the same plane as Allama Iqbal, although Bennabi remained in comparative obscurity even in the Arab world for a long time, the main reason for which seems to be his almost exclusive use of the French language for all his writings. His works have only recently been translated into Arabic. English versions of his books are still very rare. These factors contributed to the woeful lack of recognition of his due place among the Islamic thinkers of his age. The Islamic Research Institute, therefore, takes some pride in the fact that it is publishing the first English translation of one of his epoch-making works, viz. *Vocation de l'Islam*, verv ably done by Professor Asma Rashid from the original French.

Malek Bennabi was educated in Algiers and Paris, obtaining a diploma in engineering in 1952. He settled in Cairo and his exuberant mind impelled him to devote himself exclusively to writing. It was only after the heroic and persistent freedom-struggle of the Algerian people, a veritable legend of this century, humbled the arrogant obstinacy of colonial France, that Bennabi returned to his homeland in 1963 to serve as Director of Higher Education. However, he did not allow his genius to be suppressed under the weight of the onerous responsibilities of this Office and continued contributing richly to historical, cultural, philosophic and Qur'anic themes.

The *Vocation de l'Islam*, though written in 1949, was published in 1954 to synchronize with the out-break of the Algerian revolution. As the learned translator rightly observes, "the book, probably the most important of Bennabi's writings, presents an incisive and quite original analysis of the crisis facing the Muslim as well as the Western world". It is a noteworthy coincidence that the writing of Bennabi's book was almost contemporaneous with the publication of the French translation of H.A.R. Gibb's well-known work *Modern Trends in Islam* in 1949, on an almost identical theme. Bennabi's remarkable 'exposition of the twin phenomena of COLONISIBILITE and COLONISATION makes him one of the first Arab and Afro-Asian social Philosophers of our times'. His profound and masterly analysis of the politico-cultural cross-currents underlying the contemporary state of Muslim world entitles him to a position of eminence among the foremost Muslim thinkers of this century. A critical comparison of Bennabī's analysis with Gibb's appraisal of the modern trends in the Muslim world should offer an intriguing prospect to any discerning reader.

The translation was first serialized in our journal *Islamic Studies*, and has been thoroughly revised for the present volume. Miss Asma Rashid deserves the gratitude of the English readership in general, and the Islamic Research Institute in particular, for undertaking this very painstaking and scholarly task and producing a lucid translation, besides adding a number of useful footnotes, which enhance the value of this work considerably. In addition, she has contributed a comprehensive introduction, comprising a succinct account of Malek Bennabi's life and works to provide a clear perspective to the subject-matter of the book. Necessary indices have been added by our Bureau of Editing.

A change in the composing process at the Islamic Research Institute's Press compelled us to depart from our usual transliteration scheme. A table illustrating the transliteration system followed in this book has, therefore, been added.

If this translation helps in some measure to introduce a larger readership of Muslims to Bennabi's thought, we would have achieved our purpose. We hope this Institute would be able to publish the English version of some other works of Bennabi in not too remote a future.

Dr. S.M. Zaman
Director General

Islamabad
27 Rabi II 1408/19 December 1987

TRANSLATOR'S PREFACE

It is always difficult to convey faithfully the message of an author in translation, but it is even more so, in the case of Malek .Bennabi who insisted on complete accuracy and precision in the translation of his work. Anyway, I have tried my best to keep true to both the letter and the spirit of the original, at times even at the expense of strict rules of English grammar and diction. It is, of course, upto the reader to judge the result.

My thanks are due to Dr. Zia-ul Haq, former Editor, Islamic Studies, for suggesting a most apt title for the English translation.

ASMA RASHID

TRANSLITERATION TABLE

ء medial	:	'	ف	:	f
ء final	:	'	ق	:	q
ء initial	:	not expressed	ک	:	k
ا	:	a	گ	:	g
ب	:	b	ل	:	l
پ	:	p	م	:	ḿ
ت	:	t	ن	:	n
ٹ	:	t̲	ں	:	ṇ
ث	:	th	و	:	w
ج	:	j	ہ	:	h
چ	:	ch	ة	:	ah (e.g. sunnah)
ح	:	ḥ	ـة	:	at (in construct form e.g. sunnat al-Rasūl)
خ	:	kh	ی	:	y
د	:	d	ال	:	al- ('l in construct form e.g. Abū'l)
ڈ	:	d̲			
ذ	:	dh			
ر	:	r			
ڑ	:	ṛ			
ز	:	z			
ژ	:	z̲			
س	:	s			
ش	:	sh			
ص	:	ṣ			
ض	:	ḍ			
ط	:	ṭ			
ظ	:	ẓ			
ع	:	'			
غ	:	gh			

VOWELS				DIPTHONGS		
Short	ـَ	:	a	ـَو	:	aw
	ـِ	:	i	ـَی	:	ay
	ـُ	:	u	ـَے	:	ae
Long				Double		
	ـَا	:	â	ـُوّ	:	uwwa
	ـِی	:	î	ـِیّ	:	iyya
	ـُو	:	û	ـَنّ	:	anna

MALEK BENNABI:
HIS LIFE, TIMES AND THOUGHT

TRANSLATOR'S INTRODUCTION

Writing in 1949, Malek Bennabi lamented the lack of academies in the Muslim world that could establish contact and dialogue among its thinkers: "It is thus that the work of Taha Hussein has barely touched the educated milieu in North Africa and the work of Iqbal does not even find an echo therein...." The situation has hardly improved since. Few in our part of the world are really aware of the extraordinary ferment of ideas and movement that preceded and heralded the Algerian revolution, and fewer still know anything about Malek Bennabi's contribution to it as a writer, thinker and as probably the first social philosopher produced by the Muslim world since the times of Ibn-i-Khaldun.

In its duration, violence and impact, Algeria's encounter with Western colonialism was without parallel in the Muslim-Arab world. The country represented this experience not only in its tragic and painful aspects but also in its fruitful, stimulating and promising aspects and Bennabi lived this experience psychologically and ideologically with all the intensity of a highly refined and sensitive nature.

He qualified as an Electrical Engineer from a high Institute of Mechanics and Electrical Engineering in Paris and spent more than thirty years of his life in Europe. These were fertile years as regards his self-awakening and consciousness as an Arab-Muslim. Indeed his deep and intimate knowledge of Western culture and civilisation was the prime cause of his liberation from it. His scientific training, combined with a wide historical, social and philosophical outlook allowed him, on the one hand, to go to the roots of European civilisation and its hidden impulsions and motivations, and on the other, to disentangle the phenomenon of 'colonisibility' from that of 'colonisation' as the basic cause of the decadence of Muslim society. At the same time it helped him to detect the sense of history and the laws governing the march and transformation of civilisations, and to trace the new paths lying before the Muslim in the new world marching inexorably towards unity or annihilation.

As noted earlier, Bennabi was no academic scholar dealing with inanimate words in the quiet sanctuary of his study, but a writer personally involved in the drama of man and society that he sought to decipher. His thinking was born and nurtured in the misery, hunger and rags of these millions of his compatriots who lived in Algeria, a prey to the 20th century civilisation and a glaring testimony to the hypocrisy and bankruptcy of its professed ideals and objectives. This is what gives to the otherwise unembellished logic and mathematical preciseness of his words such force and radiation. For a full appreciation of his work, therefore, it would be useful as well as interesting, to be acquainted with the man, and to trace the evolution of his thought in its political, social and cultural context, by referring to his fascinating autobiographical work, *The Memoirs of a Witness of the Century**.

Bennabi was born in 1905 at Constantine in East Algeria at the moment when "the current of consciousness was connected to the past with its last witnesses, and to the future with its first architects". Perhaps nowhere was this double current so evident as in his native city and in Tebessa where the precocious child passed the formative period of his boyhood and adolescence.

The departure of his grandfather for Tripoli in the wake of the great Muslim exodus, signifying a rejection to cohabitate with the alien invaders, coincided with the death of his great-uncle, forcing his wife to restore their foster-child to his parents in Tebessa. In this extremely poor family where the father was without a job and the mother struggled to make both ends meet by her needle, Bennabi made the acquaintance of his maternal grandmother who transmitted to her grandson the vivid memories of the French entry in Constantine, bequeathed by her own mother. The little child listened intently to a recital of the tragic period when, to save the honour of the family, the Muslims had fled from the Rhumal side, letting down their young daughters by means of long ropes which at times gave way, plunging the virgins in the terrible abyss below.... Indeed, these stories and the anecdotes told by his grandmother, stressing recompense for the good action and punishment for the bad, and her emphasis on charity as the cardinal Muslim virtue, unconsciously fashioned his mind, thus deciding his future vocation in life.

In the meanwhile, Bennabi's father who possessed a Secondary School certificate, had found a job in the local Mixed Commune and so was able to send his son to the French primary school. At about this time a short trip to Constantine to see his grandfather who had been forced to return home, following the

---

* Malek Bennabi, *Memoires d'un Temoin du Siecle*, Editions Nationales Algeriennes. (Vol. I) Algiers, 1965 and Ṣhahid al-Qarn (Vol.II) Dar ul-Fikr, Beirut, 1970.

Italian landing in Libya, left a strong impression on Bennabi's mind and he began to sense for the first time the drama of history, society and civilisation that was to excite his life-long interest.

He had also imbibed a strong Turco-phile from his grandfather and passionately followed in old newspapers found at a grocer's shop, the news of the front, and of the subsequent breakup of the Ottomon empire. This did not prevent him, however, from making good progress at school, though being an indigene, was never allowed to top in class. However, he won a scholarship that would enable him to follow a two years' preparatory course at the El-Djellis school in Constantine, before joining the madrasah that prepared future Muslim justices, teachers and medical auxiliaries.

Installed in a corner of the house of his step-grandmother, Khalti Bibya, who had been forced to open her house to tenants after the death of her husband, Bennabi began his studies in earnest. His French teacher taught the eager student the art of composition and inculcated in him a passion for reading, while his Arabic teacher, drew attention to outdated bigotaries such as maraboutism and the abuses of the French administration, thus determining to a large extent, his inclinations in the intellectual order.

There was also the personal side of his life. Bennabi dearly loved his mother who had developed a spine trouble that was to leave her crippled for life. This patient, brave woman and his foster-mother instilled a lasting sweetness in his whole being. He would always recall with tenderness their unstinted love as on this occasion when his mother, on leaving after a short trip to Constantine for medical advice, turned to his foster-mother, saying:

— Bhaidja, my dear, I leave my child to you.

And Bhaidja answering in a reproachful tone:

— Oh Zahira, my dear, must you say so?

In the madrasah where Bennabi entered as a resident student, Bennabi spent most of his time either in reading French literature, especially adventure and Oriental romances, that invested him with nostalgia for the Sahara, or, in discussions with fellow-students centring at time, around Emir Khaled[1] and Ghazi Mustafa Kemal[2] whose pictures adorned the dormitories. His French teachers opened new horizons to him, including that of psychology. The Cartesian culture they imparted further helped to dissipate the fog of superstition, thus reinforcing, in a way, the reformist tendencies he had imbibed through his Arab mentors.

The works of Muḥammad 'Abduh[3] and Rashîd Raḍâ[4] exercised a determining influence on Bennabi's intellectual formation. The past richness of Muslim society made him acutely conscious of its present social distress and appalling intellectual poverty, thus saving him from a drift into romanticism, then a la mode among Algerian intelligentsia. Among the other works that left a strong impression on Bennabi and his circle, during the first two years of madrasah, were, Isabelle Eberhardt's[5] *L'Ombre chaude de l'Islam*, and Eugen Jung's[6] *l'Islam entre la baleine et l'ours*. But it was Kwâkibî[7] *Om-ul-Qura* that really produced an electrical effect on Bennabi and his friends, for, it revealed an Islam that already organised itself for defence and renaissance.

And then, late one afternoon, on the steps of the madrasah while perusing the news of the exile of Zaghloul Pasha, the Egyptian Wafad leader, Bennabi experienced with sudden and shocking clarity a new sentiment that was to serve as a goad throughout his life: He was a nationalist! He developed a passion for political reading, though only journals like *l'Humanité* could assuage his nationalist thirst. The *Iqdâm* of Emir Khalid put in his mind the first precise themes—the appalling extent of the expropriation of the Algerian fellah, the great companies that dealt in this theft and the alarming percentage of Algerian children who never went to school. His ideas took a new turn and things assumed a new significance. The sight of luxurious European villas highlighted in his eyes the growing misery of Khalti Bibya and he began to choose with the help of a friend, the house that he would occupy.

All this did not escape the notice of the French Director of the madrasah who, as a rule, preferred the apathy of the 'turbans' to the turbulence of the 'young Turks', and Bennabi's activities and reading were put under strict surveillance. But his French language teacher was more tolerant and provided him with literary journals. Through them, he came to know Tagore[8]. The latter made a strong appeal to him, mainly because he provided a comforting reassurance that it was not only on the banks of Seine or Thames that genius was born. However, his spirit carried within itself a force of recall that brought back everything that fell under his eyes to a fundamental, central pre-occupation—Islam.

All these ideas and sentiments drawn from such diverse sources were outpoured in passionate discussions in the nearby cafe Ben Yamina. Here the madrassans met the students of

Shaykh Ben Bâdis[9] who brought with them an *'ilm* politicised by the teachings of a patriotic *'âlim*. It was this conjunction of thought that was to constitute the historical prodrome of what was to be the reformist movement on one side and nationalist on the other. It was indeed, the debut of the period of psychological and social transformation to be known as *Al-Nahḍah*, the Renaissance. The Rabins Ech-Charif street, with the cafe Ben Yamina at one end and the small press of Chihab on the other, and in between the office of Ben Bâdis, became the thinking artery of the town. The growing popular participation in the debates and discussions conducted by the madrassans and the Bâdists, brought about a more solid crystallisation of progressive ideas, and the fetish respect for the "written word", that for centuries past had held the critical spirit in bondage, began to lose its hold on minds.

In this changing milieu, certain traits of Bennabi's character also began to take definite shape. While his enthusiasm for reading and discussion continued unabated, he also developed a passion for action and efficiency and an aesthetic sense, that made him revolt against all sorts of passivity and inaction as well as against disorderliness, anarchy and extremism, especially in the realm of thought and morals. At the same time, he expressed himself with a forthrightness that would earn him a reputation for inflexibility.

Alongside this ideological cleavage that created a moral frontier between those who sought a path beyond the world of marvels and those who stubbornly clung to it, Bennabi became conscious of an economic cleavage also, that had begun to operate after the end of the first World War. The old social structures were visibly dislocated, ruining an old class living on the revenue of land or traditional professions and industry, and delivering them into the clutches of Jewish moneylenders who extorted an interest of 50 or 60%, or, more often, simply obtained signature on a blank note. Between 1920 and 1925, all that had remained in the hands of the old Constantine bourgeoisie was thus liquidated. The process was the same for peasants in the surrounding areas still owning a bit of land, thus leading to a twofold transfer of property—from Algerian hands to those of Jews or Europeans, on the one hand, and from an hereditary bourgeoisie to that of commerce, on the other.

Bhaidja had already been forced to seek refuge with his family in Tebessa and each time he visited Khalti Bibya, he found her older, poorer. In the dilapidated house, he could detect old, almost sacred, souvenirs. Even in their decay, the small, materially insignificant details of the interior of Constantine houses bore witness to a certain culture and civilisation and a vague hope of the future.

He sensed the drama as acutely, in his periodic visits to his home town. Tebessa with its almost pastoral, semi-beduin ambiance and relative freedom from the colonial presence had hitherto managed to retain its soul and dignity but now, new details began to transform the physical and social scene. The great forest fires, that had swept the area towards 1912, had gradually rendered desolate the plain of Tebessa. The old families who had lived in more or less self sufficiency, found life more and more difficult and then impossible. Social degradation did, in its turn, gain the old Roman town and the last Ben Cherif was forced to abandon his ancestral home to reside in a rented room, in the dusty vicinity of the old slaughterhouse, that was to serve also as a *maktab* for teaching Quran to little boys. A steady increase in the number of Europeans, the spectacular social promotion of Jews and a more direct control of native affairs, further modified the old habitat and scene in Tebessa.

Another problem that weighed on Bennabi's mind, was that of Christianisation. One was already familiar with Father Lavigerie[10] and the means employed to christianise little Biskris and Kabyles, but with Father Zwimmer the problem acquired a new dimension. In Bennabi's eyes, Africa and Asia took on the form of a ring, with Islam and Christianity as champions, and an earnest quest for witnesses led to the discovery, among others, of Dinet, the painter of the Sahara and Grenier, the Deputy from Jura, who had embraced Islam. One heard also, for the first time of Ameer Ali's[11] *Spirit of Islam,* though no copy thereof was available either in French or Arabic.

During his last year at the madrasah, he came across Ibn-i-Khaldûn[12] and Condillace[13], the 18th century philosopher, and founded of the French school of psychology. The latter completely engrossed him, directing his mind, ideas and curiosity in a certain direction and his interest again shifted to a French bookshop. There John Dewy's[14] *How We Think* marked his first contact with American culture, while Romain Rolland's[15] *Young India* made Ghandi's name familiar. In the meanwhile, at cafe Ben Yamina, one had begun to talk excitedly of a certain Emir 'Abdel Karim[16] and his stunning victory over Spanish General Sylvester at Mililla, that shook the certainties forged at Versailles in 1919, by exposing the vulnerability of the colonial empire.

All the time, the white silhouettes of the followers of Ben Bâdis, who came from all over the country to replenish their stock of new ideas for feeding the interior, became more and more visible. Bennabi often watched this refined Constantinois, of

Sanhadja descent, on his way to or from office, but a certain reserve held him back from approaching the latter. This reserve persisted even after the battle of Iṣlâḥ was launched in earnest, and Bennabi himself was engaged in it. It was quarter of a century later, that he really recognised his error, and with his characteristic intellectual honesty, and a rare spirit of self-criticism set about to find the reasons thereof. He traced them to an ensemble of social prejudices and insufficient information on the Islamic spirit. The former, he probably inherited from his infancy in a poor family of Constantine that nourished in him, albeit unconsciously, a sort of envy or jealousy towards the big families whose issue Ben Bâdis was, while the error of judgement seemed to be the outcome of the Tebessian influence. The somewhat crude and unpolished character of Tebessa, had given him a sort of pride with regard to a more refined way of life, leading to the belief that one was nearer Islam in being closer to the *beduin* than to the *beldi* that is, the man conditioned by the urban milieu, hence, his partiality for Shaykh 'Oqbi[17] rather than Shaykh Ben Bâdis. Indeed, it was much later, that he fully recognised, why Muslim law entrusts the charge of simple *imâmat* to a man of the city in preference to a man of the tribe.

A vague sadness assailed him, as he neared the end of his final term, though previously he had looked forward to it. At this period, he could define himself politically as a revolutionary and psychologically as a conservative. As he had earlier observed while passing before the closed doors of the *zawiyas*, one becomes a contradiction in times of mutation. One destroys the past and the past clings to one. Besides, he was very sensitive to the event. Its shock could draw tears from him when, in principle, it should make him rejoice as would happen in 1940, when the Germans entered Dreux.

He began to worry, more and more, about his future. As he received no response to his various applications for a job, even in remote outposts in the Sahara, he decided, immediately after the announcement of his result, to seek his fortune in France, in the company of friend. Thus at the age of twenty, he had his first view of the sea, which appeared to him infinitely beautiful. But at Marseilles, they found themselves suddenly confronted with stark reality in the miserable looks of, mostly unemployed Algerians who constituted the reserve of French labour market for dirty or seasonal work. While two of their travel-companions, an Algerian Jew and a French-Algerian, though far less qualified, easily got work with French companies, Bennabi and his friend had no such luck, and had to sell the better part of their clothing, to keep themselves alive. Even so, they would have starved, had it not been for a providential encounter with an Algerian urchin who shared his frugal fare with them, and an

Algerian cafetier who offered them shelter and coffee. For, as Bennabi observed, despite all the disgrace that had inflicted Muslim society, Islam still maintained, therein, a sense of humanity, on a level still unattained by many civilised nations. After a month or two of harsh labour in a cementary, and, later, in a brewery, Bennabi was forced to write home for return-fare.

The end of the Rif War and the exile of Emir Khaled, dissipated his last illusions. However, happily for him, a great effervescence in ideas began to reign in Tebessa, at about the same time. The first nâdî or club came into being, and became the source of social life, where everyone took part in the decision-making process. The social spirit began to manifest itself in precise acts, such as the setting up of an independent mosque and madrasah. Thus, a new society was born in Algeria, for it is the attribute of collective consciousness and the autonomy of its decisions, that qualify a society.

At last, he gained the post of *'âdil* in the *maḥkamah* of Aflou in Oran. Here, he found himself in a rich, virgin corner of Algeria, where the country seemed to have hidden its treasure of good manners, loyalty, hospitality, love of the horse and also of its naivety. Drawing upon on his political and social experience, Bennabi tried to induce the people, still in the pastoral stage, to create social rights on the land by working it to the maximum. Otherwise, he warned, their lands would be open to confisoation, since, French law did not recognise their ownership.

But Aflou was only a charming interlude in his life. There was a torment in his soul that would not let him rest. His next appointment was at Chateaudun, where, in stark contrast to Aflou, everything had submitted to the law of colonialism. The only interest of the *qâḍî* was to augment his hectares through *bakhsheesh*, and when awarded Legion of Honour for his virtues, he had to be carted back home dead drunk. The entire cultural life of the town was summed up in endless rounds of anisette, gaming and stories of phantoms. A confrontation with the French Justice of Peace who expected servile obeisance from the indigenes, proved the last straw. Bennabi resigned his post and returned home.

He tried his hand in running a small flour-mill, in co-operation with his brother-in-law, but it flopped after a year, following the world-wide recession in 1929. Nor did he succeed in his attempt to obtain a contract for transport of road-building material. It was the summer of 1930. Bennabi stayed indoors as Algeria entered its second century of colonialism with lavish official fanfare. He had decided to leave, and his parents acquiesced in his decision, promising to defray his monthly expenses from their meagre resources.

It was autumn when he alighted in a modest hotel, situated in a small street near the Gate of St. Denis, and was greeted by the cries of call-girls, but, as he would soon discover, this was only one aspect of the life in Paris. While waiting for admission in the Institute of Oriental Studies that would allow him to join the Faculty of Law after a year, Bennabi stumbled on the centre of Christian Youth Organisation in the Trevez street and became its first Muslim member. Providentially so, as he would muse much later, for it helped him in the completion of his spiritual formation by providing answers to many of the questions that had long perplexed him. In the Trevez republic, so called because of the all-round collective life it offered to its members in its vast precincts, Bennabi found friends, belonging to different walks of life, who helped him to gain a knowledge of French life from within and facilitated his adaptation to the new milieu.

Despite good performance in the entrance examination, Bennabi failed to get admission in the Institute of Oriental Studies, since colonial policy prescribed a political rather than a scholastic criterion for an Algerian Muslim. On the advice of one of his new friends, he joined, instead, the nearby school for Wireless, and plunged himself whole-heartedly in the study of algebra, geometry, physics and mechanics. He found himself in a new world where everything submitted to the rule of 'how' and 'how much', and one learnt to value observation and exactitude. He was as fascinated by his first instrument box, that made him ponder over the evolution of a society. He saw in the Frenchman who turned into a carpenter, mechanic or painter, on returning home from work, the man of a technical civilisation who detonated the atom or sent up rockets. Even the children were reared in this direction, receiving as their first present, a set of meccano. On the other hand, in Algeria at the time, the people in the countryside possessed no instruments of repair, while the city-dwellers wasted their time in playing with cards or dominos.

Bennabi saw in school and in the street, a spontaneous link between social and technical values and those found in the Trevez republic, especially at evening prayers led by the young Director who personified the Christian spirit and the warmth of its conviction and radiation. These observations, at the same time, made him aware of aspects of his own Muslim spirit with an unwonted intensity, and led to discussion on the basic concepts of the two religions, and it was not long before it became disturbingly clear to most of the participants that the belief in Trinity could not contend with that in the oneness of God. Little did Bennabi know that colonialism did not allow freedom of thought and belief to a colonised, and that his stand was particularly serious at a moment when final touches were being given to its policy of Christianisation in North Africa.

The great colonial exhibition in Paris occupied his attention during the summer of 1931, and he saw with pain the caricature portrayal of the Muslim peoples. However, his anguish knew no bounds when he found the name of the Prophet used derisively by a wellknown commercial concern, over its stall. After vainly trying to mobilise protest against this wanton sacrilege, Bennabi returned at night to his room, sick in body and soul, and throwing himself on his bed, cried: "Oh God, they dare sully the name of thy Prophet and yet the earth does not tremble...." His words had hardly taken shape, when all at once he felt his bed rocking under him. In the morning he saw news report of an earthquake recorded at the very same hour.

As the new term began, Hamuda ben Sa'i, an old madrasah colleague whose manner of using the Quranic verse as a sociological interpretation of the present state of Muslim society had always impressed him, arrived as a student of philosophy. His constant friendship and company increased Bennabi's interest in philosophy, sociology and history, and to a great extent was instrumental in deciding his future vocation as writer specialising in the affairs of the Muslim world.

At about this time, Bennabi married a French woman. An ardent convert, she would always share, without a word of complaint, all the mental and physical trials of his life. Indeed, it is difficult to see how he would have managed to keep body and soul together without her constant love and care. With her aesthetic sense and clever fingers, she would transform the cheapest lodgings in a warm, comfortable haven, magically produce a palatable lunch out of their pitifully meagre resources, and even make him a dress when he could not afford to buy a new one. She also helped him in his thinking. For while he saw civilisational values in the things around him from a theoretical angle, she gave them a human clothing and a tangible form.

In the meanwhile, the arrival of a friend, Khalidi, from Tebessa, led to his involvement in the activities of North African students in the Latin Quarters. Bennabi gave his full support to the efforts of certain Moroccan and Tunisian students, notably, Ahmad Balfrej, Mohammad al-Fâsi and Sualeh ben Yousef to unite the North African students in order to counter the activities of a pro-government group led by a Christianised

Berber. It was in one of the meetings organised by the former, that Bennabi made his debut as a speaker. His speach, 'Why We Are Muslims?', was warmly applauded, but its consequences were disastrous for his career and family. Next day, while at the Trevez republic, he was closely interrogated by a member of the security police, and shortly afterwards received news of his father's transfer to a remote place.

His father asked Bennabi to seek the intervention of Professor Massignon[18] the official advisor on Muslim affairs, in his case. When Bennabi entered, by appointment, the study of the great scholar, the latter politely asked his permission to admit another visitor, Syed Husni. Bennabi knowing him to be the author of *Algerian Letters*, a vicious attack on Islam that had been prominently displayed at the stall of White Fathers in the Paris exhibition, impulsively exclaimed, that he did not wish to meet him. It was only afterwards that he realised that besides being a grave political mistake it was also a violent breach of etiquette. His relations with Massignon were to remain strained, hereafter.

And so, his father's transfer was not cancelled, and since his ailing wife could not accompany him to his new post, he was forced to go on leave. However, these events only hardened his attitude towards the colonial administration, and when in February 1932, Jam'iyyat al-'ulamâ' was barred from entry in mosques in Algeria, he distributed pamphlets protesting against the action. He also joined the Organisation of Arab Unity formed by Farid Zain-uddin at the behest of Emir Shakib Arslan [19] who heroically continued his struggle for Arab unity and independence from his exile in Geneva. Bennabi also co-operated with Messali Hadj[20] in the latter's attempt to resuscitate Emir Khaled's party, l'Etoile d'Afrique du Nord and its organ *al-Ummah*. But Messali's inordinate love for publicity and self-projection as *za'îm*, soon disillusioned him, and he saw with dismay leaders like him setting a new dangerous pattern for the country.

As the academic year drew to a close, his mathematics teacher, seeing his taste for theoretical studies, advised him to join the School for Mechanics Electrical Engineering. He was readily admitted by the Director of the School, who personified in Bennabi's eyes, all the attributes of a real scholar.

Bennabi had a guilty feeling about the harm he had caused to his family, but when he arrived in the summer of 1932, after a lapse of two years, he was received with open arms by his parents and two sisters. He was much relieved to find that his brother-in-law was doing well in small trade and the family had moved to more habitable quarters in the newly named Shari'

Rasool street that pointed to Tebessa's orientation as a reformist town, destined to play an important role in the coming struggle. Bennabi had already been struck by the change in the mien and deportment of the people in Algiers, the heart of colonialism in the country, and had no difficulty in tracing it to Iṣlâḥ and its centres for dissemination of Arab language and culture. The old relations between the colons and the colonised underwent a subtle change. The former began to feel that their earthly possessions were not uncontested, while the latter came to realise that pious wishes alone could not substantiate their claim to paradise.

It was during this period that Bennabi became conscious of a vague yearning, the sense of a tragedy that had haunted him in the streets of Constantine, and that could be satisfied only by drastic changes and catastrophic upheavals. In fact this feeling imbued his entire generation, or, rather the entire age, under whose feet would explode the Second World War.

At school, Bennabi worked hard to make good a five years' gap in studies. He got rid of his strong inferiority complex the day when the Director, desiring to test the level of students, posed before the class a clever question in mathematics to which Bennabi alone could provide the correct answer. However, he noted that the Director looked far from pleased and knew that even a scientist was no proof against inherited prejudices. On the other hand, Bennabi felt no constraint in his dealings with other students, both French and non-French. Among the latter was a Chinese who became a friend despite difference of opinion. While Bennabi looked upon Japan as the only hope of delivery from Western colonialism, his friend opposed Japanese imperialism itself. It was much later that he realised that this difference in opinion stemmed from the difference in their approach: for his Chinese friend viewed the problem of the colonised people from a political angle, while he himself considered it from a civilisational viewpoint.

The music in the Arab countries slowly took on the note of nationalism. Bennabi saw with consternation his own country's drift towards noisy demonstrations and government manipulated elections. He looked upon it as barren and harmful for it drove unschooled minds to indulge in imaginary struggles and dramatic heroics. It was wrong to claim that these were necessary steps in the awakening of the people, for the grinding struggle they had already waged under the standard of Iṣlâḥ had already made them conscious of their problems. Far from accelerating the march of the people towards the revolution, the political parties actually delayed it till after the war. Indeed, Bennabi believed Messali Hadj responsible for many of the pitfalls faced by the country after its independence.

In the meantime, Iṣlâḥ followed a precarious path between the two wings of Algerian nationalism—that of the working class with bourgeois aspirations headed by Messali Hadj and linked to the Left in France, and the bourgeois wing, product of Western education, led by Farhat Abbas[21] and collaborating with the French Right. Bennabi believed, and time only strenghthened his belief, that a social system can rest only on moral foundations, and saw with dismay the *'ulamâ'* handing over the keys of popular life to the elected members. For, the *'ulamâ'*, on their part, had no experience of the means employed by colonialism in the ideological struggle, and lacked the incisiveness of spirit and boldness of will, even to take note of this deviation and to make a stand against it. As Bennabi sadly recognised, Iṣlâḥ did not mean the same thing to a mind trained in the cartesian logic and that shaped by *'ilm-al-kalâm*. Later on, he would try to seek, from a civilisational angle, the causes of this failure on the part of the *'ulamâ'*, that is, a party fashioned by the traditional culture, to face their responsibilities in moments of crisis.

Bennabi had not told the family about his marriage, but her mother somehow knew, and during his short trip home the previous year had asked him to bring his wife when he came again. Now, as the school term was drawing to a close, he received a telegram asking for an immediate presentation of his wife. But when they arrived a month later, it was too late. It was an overwhelming loss and for years Bennabi would wake up at night crying for the dear beloved woman who had meant so much in his life.

The year 1934 was marked also by far-reaching events in Algeria and elsewhere. The refusal of the French President to receive an all-party delegation and the resulting wave of resignations that stunned the administration; the growing arrogance and intransigence of the Jewish community that sparked off the first Jewish-Muslim riots in Constantine and the rising political tempo in Morocco and Tunisia, following the return of Maghrebian students armed with degrees,—all pointed to a spiritual change in various directions. On the international plane, Najashi's appeal for help, fell on deaf ears, the Spanish civil war was in full swing, the Germans occupied Saar and the Zionist movement gained growing support among Western political and journalist circles.

Unable to concentrate on his studies and weary of faces and horizons in colonial and colonised territory, Bennabi decided to seek his fortune in Ḥijâz. He knew already that his stand on Zionism, and predilection for Islam, Wahhabism, nationalism and technology, would disqualify him for a job in France and for quite some time had been planning to set up an independent plant in that country, while his wife would start a centre for teaching girls needlework and poultry-farming. He was elated to get the passports, but at the last moment was denied an Egyptan transit visa, needed for change of ship at Suez. It made him realise the fact that in certain circumstances, colonialism prefers to retain the semblence of legality while relying on its lackeys in the Muslim world to do the dirty job. His disappointment was all the more galling, since a Jewish school fellow of East European origin, had just got a job in Egypt as an engineer, on the advice of the country's consul.

However, his mischance led him to resume his studies. He made good progress in theoretical studies and learnt that equations were the key to technical implementation. At the same time, he kept in touch with Algerian politics and was always ready to use his tongue or pen to defend the cause of truth and freedom, thus inviting surveillance of security services as well as of church authorities, always ready to accuse Islam of complicity whenever the international climate turned turbid.

It was May 1937. Bennabi worked far into the night for his final examination and so, in the morning had to be awoken by his wife. One morning, however, he found himself fully awake with the sparrows and their pet cat and suddenly became conscious of a turning point in his life. He would soon pass out as an engineer and his pen had already proved its worth. He stood at the threshold of a life of fame and and success. And then, suddenly, something seemed to well up within him and he found himself strangled with tears and saying again and again: "Ah! no, my God, my God, I do not want my portion in this world." Many a time, while treading the long weary path of a life planted with all sorts of thorns, Bennabi would break down and implore God not to hold him to the letter of his words.

Examinations were over, and Bennabi was free to devote more attention to the affairs of his country. He and his friends had hailed the holding of the Algerian Muslim Congress in June 1936, for they regarded it as the greatest victory scored by the people over itself and over the forces that were determined to keep it in the mud. However instead of guarding this victory and continuing the struggle on the native soil, it was decided to transfer it to the land of the adversary, where it dissipated its force in empty fanfare.

Then, one day, he received a letter from his school. Its contents would for ever remained engraved in his memory: "...The Secretariat of the School for Mechanics and Electricity warns you that you fail to fulfill, in certain particulars, the conditions for the examination..." The shock that these words produced was as much due to the destruction of all his hopes as to its moral bearing. For he believed in the moral value of science and saw it personified in the Director. Now, in a moment, his faith in science and men of science was shattered.

But this was not the only blow dealt by fate during that period. From Algeria news came of the murder of the official *muphti* of Algiers, and its ascription to the Jamiat-i-'Ulema. It was followed by a statement by Dr. Bendjelloul, the President of the Muslim Congress that amounted to an official endorsement of the official position. It was not merely a stab in the back of the Reformist movement but also of the sacred unity of popular forces, gained after quarter of a century's struggle.

In France, the Rightists hailed the victory of Franco, while the Progressists, who never cared a straw for the plight of the Algerian workers, legally their co-citizens, mobilised all their resources in aid of the Spanish refugees. This comparison, in the context of a chain of other experiences, led Bennabi to conclude that human relations are not fashioned in accordance with objective laws but are born among the individuals of a society whose destiny has been demarcated by history as a 'whole'. During this period, he spent a lot of time with his mother-in-law, a war-widow re-married to a farmer in Dreux. Like so many of their age group, they lived on their savings and modest investments, while making themselves useful through poultry farming. Bennabi fully availed this rare opportunity to study the true face of French civilisation, rooted in the countryside, wherein the relation between man and soil was fashioned in the course of the centuries. He was also amazed to find that his wife and her mother knew the names of all the plants and the insects, for in Algeria, the educated people labelled all plants as 'plant' and all insects as 'insect'. These observations on the schematisme that puts its imprint on the formulation of thought in the Muslim countries, turned his attention to the great difference between culture and education. A study of Balzac[22], whose works he found in his mother-in-law's small kitchen library, provided him further information on French life as it moved into the industrial age. These observations and comparisons fed his nascent social thinking and led to fruitful discussions with his friends in Paris. He also tried his best though with little success, to direct the attention of the Algerian students, whom he saw with concern riding the Messali bandwagon, to the basic problem of psychological and social transformation as an essential prerequisite for the formation of a polity.

Meanwhile all his efforts to find a job in France or to get a visa, even for Italy and Afghanistan, proved fruitless. It hurt him greatly that instead of supporting his family, he was still a burden on his father. Winter was changing to spring, but the storm within his soul cast its shadow over everything. Like a prisoner within his cell, Bennabi began to live within himself. The colonial fact seemed to act as a barrier between him and his friends from the Trevez republic. Even a contract to act as a salesman for a Parisian publishing concern, in Algeria ended in failure. He found all doors barred to an Algerian Muslim, all the more suspect in French eyes because he could speak their language better than themselves. He gave up after a few days' struggle, and moved on to Tebessa.

The social scene in Tebessa appeared to him as arid and barren as the land that had once been lush green. One no longer sensed the collective bond between hearts and minds on social issues which, in turn, were lost in a deluge of empty words. For, to aggravate the situation, the Popular Front, exercising the same influence on Algerian life, in general, as it had exercised in France, opened the floodgates of words. Every one seemed to be afflicted with this disease. One of these afflicted individuals was seen, at a meeting, demanding that he must be allowed to speak, else, he would burst; when given the platform, the patient, brandishing a broom, shouted, "we must sweep away colonialism with this", and sat down, relieved and happy. This pulverisation created a congenial climate for the implantation of Messali Hadj's party in the capital and elsewhere. Thus, the country abandoned the arena of duties, and moved towards the field of 'rights' and 'progress', oblivious of the growing misery of the people, their heart-rending poverty, sickness and starvation.

The weakness or inability of the 'ulamâ' to counter this fatal love for demonstration, encouraged and exploited by colonialism, contributed to wreck the Muslim Congress. Colonialism scored another victory, in the strict field of Iṣlâḥ itself, when under its blessings, the President of the defunct Congress formally reinstated the rites and customs, that the people had renounced two years ago.

One day, Bennabi learned from a friend, who had remained faithful to him in an atmosphere wherein everyone who wanted to gain or maintain the favour of the administration avoided him, that a club formed in Marseille to educate Algerian workers, was in need of a teacher, and lost no time in offering his services. He would always remember the introductory remarks of one of the founder-members, who told the workers that the new teacher was bearer of a light which they must seek to preserve. He looked on these words as the first response of the

Algerian people to the cruel treatment that he and his family had received at the hands of colonialism. And when he, himself spoke to the workers and saw the signs of misery fade even from the starved faces of the unemployed, he felt triumphant like a man emerging from a grave wherein he had been entombed alive. He was to experience this sensation, time and again, in a life of continuous struggle against heavy odds.

Without a thought for renumeration, Bennabi plunged himself whole-heartedly in his new duties. There was to be a weekly class and assembly. The latter posed no difficulty, because, he was used to discussing even complex social issues in the language of the people. However, the arrangement of lessons for students differing greatly in age, mental capacity and social background, was not so easy. His youngest student was a lad of seventeen from the Kabyles, while in the first (row) he noticed a tall, handsome man, well advanced in years. Bennabi was startled to know that his name was Tashfin Abdullah and that he came from Tlemcen. Was it possible that this man driven to the streets of Marseille in his old age, was a scion of Yusuf ben Tashfin, the founder of the Murabit state in Maghrib? On inquiry, the man stated that he used to teach Quran to the children, but as it did not enable him to feed his family, he was forced to leave his home. These simple words were a poignant reminder of the cruel transformation imposed by colonialism in Algeria. Bennabi had already seen the effects of this tragedy, in the home of Khalti Bibya, and now saw it personified, with staggering clarity, in the person of Tashfin Abdullah, though the man himself was hardly conscious of it.

Bennabi finally decided to follow a novel method of teaching. While imparting basic knowledge of reading and writing, he would try to bring about a change in the mental dimensions of his students, through a confrontation with infinity. Now one could enter the realm of infinity, besides religion, through big numbers or astronomy. Bennabi chose a short cut through numbers, and geography— the smaller door of astronomy. He was delighted to find that, after only a few sessions, students who could not write even upto ten, could easily write billions and trillions and solve simple mathematical problems of four numbers. Equally explosive in its impact, was the introduction of a world wall-map. The students moved from 'how many' to 'how', that is, to the differences between men and civilisations and thence to discussion on politics and morality, especially behaviour. Bennabi exhorted his students to look after their appearance and to develop a love for cleanliness and order. He could notice after a few months, the change in their mental attitudes reflected in their faces, thus discovering that civilisation not only puts its imprint on the world of things but also bestows traits of beauty on the faces of men.

But this sweet aspect of his life did not extend to its material side, where his wife who since her arrival had quite naturally assumed the duties of a mother, doctor and apothecary for the students, alone bore the burden. For, it was not long before the Centre became a target of attack both from colonial and the Messalist quarters, and the contributions for it dwindled away. Meanwhile the world was slowly sliding towards the abyss of war and tensions had reached a breaking point. On Sept, 28, 1938, the Leftist-Progressist parties organised a joint meeting. Speaking on behalf of his Centre, Bennabi proposed that the meeting should call on government to grant to the peoples of North Africa their legitimate rights so that they could enter the struggle for democracy as dignified partners rather than as mere mercenaries. But though widely applauded, his proposals found no mention in the final draft resolution. For the so-called progressive forces that posed as the champions of the North African people, merely wanted to exploit the immigrant workers as a shield in their confrontations with the government or other parties.

However, Bannabi repeated his demand before a large gathering of Algerian workers. A few days later, he was summoned to the Marseille Academy and ordered to close his school on the ground that it had no proper building and he did not possess a teaching certificate. When Bennabi politely asked for the real reason, he was told that it was the Palestine affair that had created difficulties for the administration of native affairs!

Back in Tebessa, he found the current of oratory still running strong, while Messalist cells riddled the country. However, despite desertions from its ranks, the Iṣlâḥ remained the primary preoccupation of the colonial authorities and one day, Shaykh Arabi al-Tabissi was summoned before the city administrator and curtly told: You want to revive the Qur'ân while we wish to bury it.

Bennabi's only activity consisted in delivering lectures before a listless audiance in the *nâdî* and so, when Shaykh Arabi asked him to translate into French an excellent study of the role of the Jews in the fashioning of the modern world, entitled *al-Ṣirâ'* by an exiled Saudi writer, and also to write an introduction thereof, he readily agreed. But when he had completed his assignment with his usual thoroughness the Shaykh asked him to modify his introduction for he was certain that the administration would not allow its publication. Bennabi argued that they should not help the administration in the performance of its duties, by witholding the publication, but without avail. He realised then that an educated Muslim, whatever his orientation, if he did not find any obstacles in his way tended to create them himself.

The war burst at last and house searches began. Bennabi buried the article on Palestine and on 22nd September took the ship for France, vowing to return only to an independent homeland. *

The war in Europe further aided him in his diagnosis of the Western civilisation and its growing bankruptcy. In his eyes, Nazi barbarism was merely an extension of the colonial spirit in the heart of colonialism itself. The Setif massacre of May 1945 in Algeria and the brutal suppression of freedom movements elsewhere, most tragically in Palestine, by the self-same Powers that claimed to be the standard-bearer of the 'free world', strengthened his belief that the path to dignity and freedom did not lie in clamourous demonstrations or fabricated elections. The battle against Colonialism must be fought not only on the political and military fronts but also on the ideological front, and as a first step, one must try to comprehend the twin phenomena of colonisibility and colonialism. It was essential to find out the root-cause of the malaise that for centuries had immobilised Muslim society, while at the same time, it was necessary to acquire the capability to detect and foil all colonial moves to deflect the people from the path of revolution.

And Bennabi undertook this formidable and thankless task with the objectivity of a scientist and the faith of a visionary. We find him henceforth fully engaged in the struggle for freedom, tackling the obstacles that hindered its march, defining its goals, tracing an active path for it, clearing horizons obscured by the colonial mist, and providing to the culture his generation a basis drawn from its own history and moral values.

It was in the latter context that his first great work, *The Quranic Phenomenon* (French) was published in Algiers in 1946. Bennabi knew that the framework of classical exegesis must be drastically revised and broadened, in order to resolve the crisis of faith that confronted Muslim youth trained in cartesian modes of thought and forced to depend on Western Orientalists for an appreciation of Islam. The Muslim exegetists had hitherto

---

* Bennabi's Memoirs cover the period from 1905 to 1939. The rest of the account is derived from his other writings.

relied almost exclusively on *bayan* — a discipline on the cross-roads of rhetoric and stylistic, in their effort to provide rational basis for the Quranic miracle. Bennabi showed the way to a re-formulation of the classical exegesis by introducing a new methodology that would benefit from new fields of science, such as astro-physics, psychology and archeology. The book, while raising a hue and cry in traditionalist circles, was widely acclaimed by the Muslim-Arab intelligentsia, as a much-needed pioneering effort in the field, and established Bennabi's reputation as a noteworthy Muslim scholar.

His next publication was *Labbayk* (Arabic, Algiers, 1947), his first and only novel which already bore the stamp of his social thinking. But his next important contribution was, *The Conditions of the Renaissance* (French, Algiers, 1948). While dealing with various aspects of the Algerian problem, the book reflects the main themes of Bennabi's social philosophy that were to find full expression in *Vocation de l'Islam* (French, Paris, Edition Du Seuil, 1954),presented, herewith, under the title, *Islam in History and Society*.

In this book, the author does not bother himself with a record of events or details, but from the outset concentrates on a methodical analysis of the various stages of history and the march and evolution of civilisation. Developing further the notion of cycle inherent in Ibn-i-Khaldûn's theory of *'aṣabiyyah,*Bennabi presents his own theory of the cyclical phenomenon, according to which civilisation perpetuates itself in an indefinite exodus, through successive metamorphoses, each of them being a particular synthesis of man, soil and time. In the light of the above, he divides the history of Muslim society in three stages: The first, representing at its most sublime, the impulsion and living force of Qur'ân ended with the battle of Ṣiffîn; the second witnessed the flowering of Muslim culture and civilisation and lasted till the fall of the al-Muwaḥḥids; while, the third, denotes the period of stagnation and decadence. Since Muslim society continues to be bogged down in its sedimnts, the last stage receives special attention.

At this point in his historical analysis, Bennabi turns to the European world and looks into the origins and evolution of its civilisation, and its formative elements—the organised materialism stemming from an agrarian milieu, Christianism that endowed its static temperament with dynamism and the ferment of moral expansionism that was to serve as justification for the Crusades, and later, the colonial enterprise, and Cartesianism that prepared it for an efficient integration in the great industrial upsurge, and finally led to a perversion of moral and human values and their connation.

The author presents the dramatic confrontation between these two worlds at a turning point in history. The departure of its civilisation has left the one a calcified skeleton, its breath of living faith frozen in hollow words—a world that has become 'colonisable' before being colonised, while in the other, civilisation has completed its course, culminating in colonialism and scientism.

At this point, Bennabi provokes at once our curiosity and excitement by showing us the glimmer of a new stage of history as reflected in the re-awakening of the Muslim world and, in this connection, presents us with a critical evaluation of the traditionalist, reformist and modernist movements.

But the Muslim world cannot work out its destiny in isolation. The disintegration of the colonial and colonised worlds has laid bare the profound sense of history, revealing the basic unity of human needs and problems and the necessity of re-adjusting relations among peoples. Indeed the unity of the world has always been the essential phenomenon of history, even though it escaped the cartesian mind whose formative culture ascribes the commencement of history and thought, to the foundation of Rome and the Athenian academies. The Muslim world by its very atavism, is half-way towards this new world... Of course, the post al-Muwaḥḥid man must still attain the material level of the present civilisation, so deeply marked by the technical spirit; but his role remains, above all, spiritual, as a moderator of the accesses of modern thought and national egoism.

In the end, Bennabi makes a startling forecast: the shift of the centre of Islamic gravity from the Mediterranean to Asia, where he sees conditions most propitious for a new synthesis of man, soil and time, the formation of a popular will and evocation of that dialogue between heart and mind that he discerns in Iqbal.

During the crucial period that intervened between the completion of *Vocation de l'Islam* in 1949 and its publication in 1954, on the eve of the Algerian Revolution, Bennabi was actively engaged in expounding and elaborating his ideas in their practical application to the actual situation. In a series of articles that appeared in two French-language journals in Algiers* (published in Arabic under the title *In the Whirlwind of the Battle*, Cairo, 1961) one finds each relevant incident, each move and spoken word recorded in its political, social or ideological context, and subjected to a penetrating analysis. Nor did

* *Algerian Republic* and *Muslim Youth*

he ignore the global dimension of this struggle. On the one hand, we find him commenting on the significance of the two international conferences held simultaneously in Geneva and Colombo but with diametrically opposed objectives (1954) and on the other, asserting that the 'glimmer of hope' that Mosaddaq had brought would not be extinguished by his imprisonment or the criminal murder of Fatimi, but as in the case of the Palestine catastrophe, was bound to leave its directing influence on the history of the modern Muslim world. The 1952 Egyptian Revolution, too, excited his great interest and he saw therein the advent of a new popular consciousness that would increasingly claim the right to supervise the affairs of the state in Muslim countries.

Despite his personal and emotional involvement in events in Algeria where colonialism had launched a veritable war of extermination to crush a people's will to regain its liberty, Bennabi found time to record his reflections on the far-reaching implications of the 1955 Bandung Conference, *The Afro-Asiatism* (French), Cairo, 1956. He saw in this historic gathering, representing the major portion of humanity as well as the diversity of its ideological patrimony, not merely a novel occurence but a continuity that did, in fact, surpass the Afro-Asian perimeter, extending socially from Tangier to Jakarta and morally from Washington to Moscow, towards a two-fold fulfillment that would raise the Afro-Asian man to the social level of civilisation and the civilised man to the moral level of humanity so as to realise the unity of mankind for which the Western genius had already furnished the material conditions.

Late in August 1956, Bennabi sought political asylum in Cairo, and placed his services at the disposal of the Algerian Revolution. Though the French colonial administration through its hirelings sought to malign Bennabi and to distort his image especially in the eyes of the Algerian students, his sincerety of purpose and the force of his logic soon won him the love and confidence of the Algerian-Arab youth and intelligentsia. His anguished appeal against the French war of extermination, *S.O.S Algeria* (French) appeared in Cairo in 1957, followed in quick succession by *The Problem of Culture* (Arabic) Cairo, 1957, *The Ideological Struggle in Colonised Countries* (Arabic) Cairo, 1957, *The New Social Edification* (Arabic) Beirut, 1958 and *The Idea of an Islamic Commonwealth* (Arabic), Cairo, 1958.

In 1959, on his way to Lebanon, he visited Damascus where he was warmly received by University teachers, students and intelligentsia who were already acquainted with his work and were eager to benefit from his presence. His subsequent lectures and discourses in Damascus and Beirut are recorded in *Reflections* (Arabic) Cairo, 1960, *The Problem of Ideas in the Muslim World* (Arabic) Cairo, 1960 and *Birth of a Society* (Arabic) Cairo, 1960.

In 1963, after more than twenty years of self-imposed exile, Bennabi set foot at last, on the independent soil of his country and was appointed Director of Higher Education. He also animated a centre of Cultural Orientation, dedicated to students and participated in the establishment of Algerian national press. At the same time, he delivered a series of lectures, later published under the title *Algerian Perspectives* (French) Algiers, 1964. These lectures reflect Bennabi's growing pre-occupation with the problem of post-independence reconstruction of Muslim society and the evolvement of a precise doctrine for Muslim renaissance. Bennabi believed that the formula of Socialism, Arabism and Islamism, as inscribed in the National Charter, provided a common denominator to solve the primary question of an infra-structure. Because of its quality as a social technique applicable to the totality of the national community and, from a psychological point of view, as a factor of integration, Bennabi looked on socialism as the most efficacious operative mode, and considered far-reaching agrarian reforms as an essential first step towards a new synthesis of man, soil and time.

Bennabi is careful to point out that while in Europe the socialist movement has been marked by a two thousand years old materialist intellectual tradition, such psycho-historic factors do not intervene in Algeria or other Muslim countries; hence there is no reason or pretext to confound socialism with materialism, and its motivating force must be sought in our own traditions and spiritual resources.

The first volume of his *Memoirs* was published in 1965, followed by *The Work of The Orientalistes* (French) Algiers, 1967. The same year he resigned from his office to devote himself fully to ideological action and organisation of discussion clubs. *Islam and Democracy* (French) appeared in Algiers, 1968, followed by *The Sense of the Stage (Arabic)* Algiers, 1970 and the second volume of his Memoires (Arabic) Beirut, 1970. During this period, he also travelled widely, holding discussions and giving lectures in Egypt, Syria, Libya, Europe, United States, Indonesia, Japan and China where he was received by Mao-Tse-Tung.

His close observation of the civilisational phenomena in these countries further helped him in his search for the causes of the dismal failure of most Third World countries to realise the fruits of independence, in contrast to the remarkable post-war economic recovery of Japan and Germany and success of the revolutionary experiment in China and convinced him more than ever of the importance of ideas as instruments of evolution in a given society.

Already in 1959 Bennabi had emphasised the importance of the ideological struggle that must precede and direct the struggle for social and economic emancipation. He had further pointed to the new stage in international evolution wherein the power-struggle of the super powers had been shifted to the ideological arena, making it all the more incumbent on the Muslim and Afro-Asian countries lagging in material means of power, to devote their utmost attention to the problem of ideas.

Twelve years later, writing in his preface to the second edition of *Afro-Asiatism*, Bennabi reiterated his views on the subject. He recalled that Western international experts looked on the Bandung Conference as the most ominous development of the pos —World War II period, that had haunted Dulles to his grave and dominated Western strategy especially in the Arab world. But the Conference failed to harness its immense human and material potential for launching an effective revolt against the political, economic and social system imposed on it to serve the interests of Western imperialism, just because it lacked the ideological spark needed to trigger the required explosion. Bennabi recalled, in this connection, that one of the resolutions passed by the Cairo Conference in 1956, had called for the institution of an Afro-Asian award on the pattern of Nobel or Lenin prize. But while the Nobel prize has since been awarded 17 times, the Afro-Asian prize had not been awarded even once.

This paucity of ideas is most glaringly reflected in the economic chaos reigning in most Muslim and Third World countries whose economy is still geared to the service of world capitalism, and where, even after thirty or forty years of independence, an overwhelming majority continues to suffer from a life of degrading poverty, disease and ignorance. Bennabi devoted his attention to this basic problem, in *The Muslim in the World of the Economics* (Arabic), Beirut, 1972. His treatise shows a remarkable grasp of the subject both from an ideological and practical point of view. The author does not confine himself to an incisive analysis of the causes of economic stagnation or retrogression in the Muslim world but also presents a clear, cogent programme of economic action that, while benefiting from the experiments of other peoples, draws its inspiration from the Quranic notion of social justice and human dignity.

His mission was now nearing its end. On his way back to Algeria, from his last pilgrimage in the early summer of 1972,

Bennabi delivered two lectures in Damascus on *The Role of the Muslim in the Last Third of the 20th Century* (published in Arabic, Damascus, 1973).

He spoke of the momentous crisis that today faced the Washington-Moscow axis, that is the axis of power, science and civilisation, and traced it to a loss of old justifications that had hitherto motivated and validated its ideological, social and economic life, and the failure of subsequent efforts to replace them. It is this fatal vacuum, this absence of a raison d'etre that is driving the flower of its youth to desperation, on the path of bestiality, drugs and suicide.

History seems to have reached once again a point of no return, and Bennabi believed the moment to be ripe for the final realisation of the Quranic verse: It is He, who has sent His Apostle with Guidance and the Religion of Truth, that he may proclaim it over all religions. (21:28)

But the Muslim can fulfil his mission only if he first fulfilled its conditions. Before saving others, he must first save himself. He must raise himself to the level of civilisation and above it, so as to raise civilisation to the sanctity of existence, the divinity of existence, that cannot exist apart from the existence of God.

And thus this great Muslim fighter continued his life-long *jihâd* against superstition, bigotary, and mental and physical slavishness. Never afraid to look reality in the face, he forever engaged himself on the side of truth and justice. His force of expression showed no sign of slackening and his determination to expose all falseness and hypocrisy never faltered, till he breathed his last on October 31, 1973.

May his soul rest in peace!

ASMA RASHID

NOTES AND REFERENCES

1. The grandson of Emir Abd-al-Qadir, and the veritable precursor of Algerian nationalism who spoke of Algerian independence as early as 1926. Died in exile in 1937.
2. Ataturk (1881-1938)
3. Muḥammad ʻAbduh (1830-1876) Egyptian writer, theologian and initiator of Muslim reformism.
4. Muḥammad rashîd Raḍâ, (1865-1935) Lebanese scholar, theologian and reformer. Author of *Tafsîr al-Manâr*
5. *The Warm Shadow of Islam*. A bohemian enamoured of the Sahara who tragically met her death at Ain-Sefra.
6. *Islam between the Whale and the Bear*. The author died twenty years later in a Parisian garret, ignored and forgotten by all.
7. ʻAbd-al-Raḥmân b. Masʻûd al-Kwâkabî (1849-1902) Syrian writer and thinker. His other important work is titled *Ṭabâ'iʻ al-Istibdâd.*
8. Rabindranath Tagore (1861-1941) Indian nationalist writer and poet belonging to W. Bengal.
9. ʻAbd al-Ḥamîd b. Muḥammad Bin Bâdîs (1887-1940) Algerian writer, theologian and reformer. As the founder-President of Jamʻiyyat al-Muslimîn (1931) and editor of *al-Shahâb*, played an important and far reaching role in the Algerian struggle for independence.
10. Charles Lavigerie (1825-1892). The Archbishop of Algeria who founded the Order of African Missionaries, known as White Fathers.
11. Syed Amir Ali, Indo-Pakistani jurist and writer (1849-1928). As could be seen from the above, *The Spirit of Islam*, a liberal and modernist interpretation of Islam, exercised an influence in the Muslim world that extended far beyond the sub-continent.
12. ʻAbd al-Raḥmân Ibn Khaldûn (1332-1406), The great Arab historian and sociologist born in Tunis.
13. Étienne Bonnot De Condillac (1714-1780) French philosopher and master of the sensualist school. Author of the *Traité des sensations* and of *Logique*.
14. American philosopher and pedagogue (1859-1952)
15. French writer (1866-1944). His cult of heroes animates his historical and philosophical dramas, His idealised picture of Gandhi seems to have left a lasting impression on Bennabi's mind.
16. The Rif leader (1882-1963), who victoriously led his people in their revolt against Spanish domination but was everwhelmed by French military might in 1926.
17. Taiëb al-Okbi was a prominent member of the Ulema movement, from the region of Biskra. But his persecution on a trumped up charge of complicity in the murder of the efficial mufti of Algiers (August 1936) badly shook him. He formally parted ways with Ben Badis in 1939 and affirmed his loyalty to France.
18. Louis Massignon (1883-1962). French orientalist and author of many important works on Islamic mysticism.
19. Lebanese thinker, writer and reformer and editor of the journal *La Nation Arabe* (1869-1946)
20. A little cultivated, ex-army man, Messali Hadj was a born speaker and organiser. Bennabi's misgivings about him were fully realised. His inordinate love for self-projection prevented him from joining forces with F.L.N when the November 1954 revolution broke out, and, ultimately he became a tool of the French policy to stir up internecine strife in Algerian ranks in order to arrest the march of the revolution.

21. A pharmacist by profession, Farhat Abbas (1900–1986) was an ordent supporter of French–Algeria, but was finally disillusioned by french colonial policy. Joined F.L.N in April 1956 and became chairman of the Provisional Government of Algeria set up in 1958.
22. Honoré De Balzac (1799–1850) French writer and author of the *Human Comedy* that presents a veritable fresco of the French society of the Revolution at the end of the July monarchy.

INTRODUCTION

The outline of my work was ready when I came to know of Gibb's *Modern Trends in Islam.*[1] On many points his position resembles mine.—Should I, then, have merely asked the reader to refer to him? On the contrary, despite the similarities, I decided to follow my own path. I also want to point out certain divergences.

Thus I do not believe that atomism — the turn of mind which is incapable of generalisations—is a specific characteristic of the Arab mind, as Gibb contends. It is rather a question of the modality of human spirit in general when it has not yet attained a certain degree of development and intellectual maturity, or has passed it by. More precisely, the discursive spirit inscribes itself, in the historical evolution, between two stages of atomism. Thus thought is necessarily "atomistic" in its first take-off, as was the case in Europe in the pre-Cartesian period, and becomes so again when all intellectual effort ceases, as in the post-Khaldûnian period in the Muslim world.

But the important cultural heritage that the Muslim civilization has bequeathed to modern civilization, bears witness to an altogether different turn of Muslim spirit during the periods of its flowering. Its labour was, in fact, marked in all fields by a sense of "law" which pre-supposes the aptitude to synthesise. The Muslim law offered for the first time in history the aspect of a philosophical system developed on the basis of fundamental principles, while Roman law constituted merely an empirical compilation of legal recipes.

One could also point out, in astronomy, Abû'l Wafâ's[2] discovery of the "variation" or second inequality of the movement of moon, or to recall that it is Ibn Khaldûn to whom belongs the honour of being the first to have disentangled the laws of history and their relations with the activities of societies.

We do not share either the views of the English scholar on the "humanist tendency" which he rightly discerns in the Muslim modernist movement, but which he imputes to the influence of European culture.[3]

One must be clear about the terms. If it is a question of an academic or diplomatic humanism, we readily acknowledge that modern humanistic phraseology is superb, and that certain slogans or well-turned out phrases may have "enriched" the baggage of certain Muslim modernists. But one should, perhaps, examine facts rather than words, and confront "humanism" with its real attributes: tolerance, altruism and respect for human person.

One would not, on this point, engage in a comparison that would be out of place here and which must start, in so far as it concerns Islamic humanism, by a recourse to the "religious value" which the Qur'ân accords to the individual, as we have already discussed in our study *Le phenomene coranique*[4] (the chapter: Rapport Coran-Bible); then, Abû Bakr's exhortation to the Muslim army enjoining upon it to respect the "unarmed, the monk, the cattle and plantation". (We are far from the methods of war of the so-called civilised countries.) Also, the significant attitude of ʿUmar on entering Jerusalem: he refused to cross the threshhold of the Temple, and contented himself with posing thereon his head respectfully thus guaranteeing it to the Christians, against the audacity of Muslim soldiers. One cannot help thinking also of the liberalism of Muslim science that in the period of its "euphory" unconditionally offered itself to human mind. The Mongol mercenary who accompanied Chengiz Khan could as liberally benefit from it as the monk Gerbert[5] or the talmudist Maimonides.[6] When one thinks, on the other hand, of the sort of the haughty donation that the present European civilisation makes of its science to the "backward" countries,—or more exactly, to the countries it has made backward—one finds it difficult to forget that certain Muslim intellectuals have had to pay its price by years in prison. Why would the Muslim, in these circumstances, seek to find inspiration for its humanism elsewhere than in his own millenarian tradition?

There apparently remains the possibility of defining a centripetal humanism: in this case, it signifies "Europeanism" within and "colonialism" without—the latter based on the most scandalous and most odious political equation according to which a *man* multiplied by *coloniser co-efficient* is equal to an *indigène*."[7]

Howsoever that may be, the work of the English scholar deserves full attention of the Muslim for taking a true stock of his ideas and for estimating objectively not only the values of his renaissance but also the "non-values" which currently form the essential elements of the chaos of the Muslim world. Gibb points out, in particular, the "literalism" that we had believed to see denounced under the term of "alphabetism".

Of no less interest to those who regard "truth" as the motor and index of progress, is Gibb's vigorous exposition of the "apologetique" taste and romanticism that mark our culture even among certain great modern minds. The "apologetique" is a betrayal of this truth, and through it, of history itself.

But if one betrays truth by overestimating oneself, one does so also by under-estimating oneself. In this regard, Gibb seems to have omitted to note the inferiority complex of certain Muslim intellectuals and leaders.

I would repeat that the book of the English scholar provides a precious guide on the plane of what may be called the pathology—quasi-infantile—of the Muslim world. I hope that its themes would be meditated upon by many Muslims, sensible, like myself, of the honesty of thought that could manage to liberate itself from all confessional or political complexes.

TRANSLATOR'S NOTES

1. The English edition of Gibb's *Modern Trends in Islam* was published in 1947 (viz. H.A.R. Gibb, *Modern Trends in Islam*, Chicago: University of Chicago Press, 1947), but Bennabi is obviously referring to its French translation published in 1049. (trad. fr. de B. Vernier, Paris: G.P. Maisonneuve, 1949).

2. Abû'l-Wafâ' (940-997 A.D.) was a great Arab mathematician.

3. It is with particular reference to Iqbâl's philosophy that Gibb makes the above assertion: "All unconsciously, Iqbâl was importing into Islam the same tendencies in thought as have in the West, been gradually transforming Christianity into a religion of humanism..." Gibb, *op. cit.* (English edition), pp. 81-82.

4. Algiers: *En-Nahda*, 1946.

5. Gerbert, who spent several years in Spain prior to his becoming Pope Silvester II (999-1003), introduced Arabic numerals to the West. P.K. Hitti, *History of the Arabs* (London: McMillan), p. 574.

6. Mûsâ ibn Maymûn (1135-1204), the most famous of the Hebrew physicians and philosophers of the entire Arab epoch. (*Ibid*, pp. 584-85).

7. The term *idigène* (native) as used by Bennabi is expressive of the glaring inequities that the Algerian Muslim suffered under the *indigenat* system, based on the colonial dictum, affirmed by the Superior Council of Algeria early in 1894, that the "Arab is an inferior race incapable of being educated". Charles Andre Julien, *L'Algerie Contemporain* (Paris: Julliard, 1972), p. 31.

●●●

1

THE POST AL-MUWAHHID SOCIETY

"That people have now passed away;
They have the reward of their deeds ..."
QUR'ĀN (2:134)

1

1. THE CYCLICAL PHENOMENON

"We alternate the days of successes and Reverses among peoples..."

Qur'ân (3:140)

One could consider the historical phenomenon from various points of view: from the point of view of the individual, it is above all a *psychology*, that is, a study of man regarded as a psycho-temporal factor of a civilization. But this civilization is the manifestation of a life and collective thought. From this point of view, history is a *sociology*, that is, the study of the conditions of development of a social group, defined not as much by its ethical or political factors as by the complex of ethical, aesthetical and technical affinities corresponding to the *aire*, or space, of this civilization. On the other hand, this social group is not isolated, and its evolution is conditioned by certain connections with the human ensemble. From this point of view, history is a *metaphysics*, since its perspective, extending beyond the domain of historical causality, embraces the phenomena in their finality.

In a preceding study, we had approached the subject from the point of view of the individual, in order to highlight the conditions that the latter must offer to the development of a civilization of which he is necessarily the decisive factor. Now we shall adopt the last two points of view for studying the modern evolution of the Muslim world, while pointing out the effective or possible connections of this evolution with the general movement of human history.

It is difficult to know the origins of this movement in space and time, and it will not serve any purpose to enquire if it commenced in Egypt or elsewhere. One can only ascertain its *continuity* through the ages. Whenever one has attempted to establish its "historical" co-ordinates, one perceives that they designate a space that changes its place. So that the continuity that one ascertains in the general perspective of history, could find itself masked by a *discontinuity* that appears when one looks upon the succession of the spaces or areas of civilization. In fact, we find, there, the two essential aspects: the metaphysical or cosmic, that of a general design, of a finality; and the properly, sociological "historical", aspect, that of an enchainment of causes.

One must add that under this last aspect, civilization presents itself as a numerical series following its course in similar but non-identical terms. Thus appears an essential notion of history: the *cycle of civilization*. Each cycle is defined by certain psycho-temporal conditions proper to a social group: it is a "civilization" in these conditions. Then the civilization migrates, shifts its abode, transfers its values in another area. It thus perpetuates itself in an indefinite exodus, through successive metamorphoses: each metamorphosis being a particular synthesis of man, soil and time.

But it often happens that one truncates the historical conception, as did Thucydides[1] who annulled the entire past of humanity by declaring that before his epoch "no important event was produced in the Universe". It is thus that one creates the *culture of the empire*, entailing the myths of the dominant race and the civilising mission of colonialism. The Marxist thought also neglects the essential notion of cycle by its assertion that "the social and historical processes move from the era of primitive animality' to the era of abundance, consciousness and liberty"—even though the finalism implied in this perspective is contradicted by the very principle of the *dialectic*.

It was Ibn Khaldûn who, inspired probably by Islamic psychological factors, disentangled the notion of cycle in his theory of the "three generations", wherein the terminology, somewhat summarised, masks the profoundness of the idea by reducing the dimensions of a civilization to the scale of the dynasty, *'aṣabiyyah*. Even if narrow, this conception invites us to emphasize the transitory aspect of civilization, that is, to see in the latter only a succession of organic phenomena, each of which necessarily possesses in a determined space a beginning and an end. The importance of this conception lies in that it allows one to discuss not only the conditions of progressive development but also the factors of regression and decadence: the force of inertia of a civilization. It permits us to embrace a whole whose phases are not independent: in a biological process these are the causes of life and death—internal contradictions—that lead the being to its full development and then to its final disintegration. In the social order this fatality is limited or rather conditioned, because the direction and the term of evolution depend on the psycho-temporal factors on which an organised society could, in a certain measure, act by regulating its life and pursuing certain ends in a coherent manner.

All these considerations lead us to condemn the habit of regarding in isolation a phenomenon "civilization" and a phenomenon "decadence". On this point, the Muslim world is particularly in need of clear ideas that would guide its present effort of renaissance.

In the first place, it is important to be fully conscious of the remote causes that have determined its decadence. The Muslim world knew its first rupture at the battle of Ṣiffīn, in the year 37 of the *Hijrah,* since it already contained—so soon after its birth—an internal contradiction: the Jâhilî spirit contending with the Qur'ânic spirit. It was, moreover, Muʿâwiyah, who broke a synthesis—in principle established for a long time, perhaps for evermore, thanks to the equilibrium between the spiritual and the temporal.

From this first rupture to which we would revert again, even if the Muslim could live fundamentally attached to a spiritual order contained within his believing soul, the Muslim world did, nevertheless, lose its first equilibrium. Yet, it is evident that we owe to this deviated *civilization* that flourished at Damascus under the Umayyads, the discovery of the decimal system, application of the experimental method, notably in medicine and the introduction of the mathematical notion of time,* which form the first landmarks of technical thought. One would, perhaps, even find one day that the "apple of Newton"—that would reveal to this illustrious astronomer, the universal attraction—is not without some relation with the works of Ibn Mûsâ brothers.** However, from a bio-historical point of view that concerns us, all this brilliant civilisation was but a denaturalisation of the original synthesis realised by the Qur'ân and founded on the equilibrium of spirit and reason, on the two-fold moral and material base, necessary for all durable social edifice.

In reality, the Muslim world could only survive this first crisis in its history because of what remained in it of the impulsion and living force of the Qur'ân. It were men like ʿUqbah, ʿUmar ibn ʿAbd al-ʿAzîz, and Imâm Mâlik, who maintained it, not because one was a great conqueror, the other a great monarch, and the third the head of a juridical school; but because they incarnated under different titles, the simple and great virtues of Islam.

---

*The Arabs were the first to utilise "equal hours". Before them, the Greeks and the Roman had divided time into two unequal periods: 12 hours for the day and 12 different hours for the night.

The elder, Muḥammad ibn Mûsâ ibn Shâkir, who wrote, notably, a "Treatise on the Power of Attraction", died in 873 A.D.

In the vicinity of the future Fâṭimid capital,* whence the Muslim army set out for the conquest of North Africa, ʿUqbah, who had just embraced his children for the last time, cried, while getting astride his horse: "Oh God! call my soul! "Later on, ʿUmar ibn ʿAbd al-ʿAzîz, judging it unjust to withhold a power which seemed to him to belong to the descendants of ʿAlî, preferred to renounce it; and Mâlik offered himself in the public squares of Madinah, to the floggings of an oppressive power whom his teaching disavowed. These are the virtues,— this contempt for the glory that presented itself; this refusal of the power that seemed undue, and defiance opposed to it, when it became unjust—that have sustained in the Muslim world the ferment of life deposed in it by the Qur'ân.

One could understand the value that the great sociologist (that was) Muḥammad attached to the moral virtues as the essential force of civilizations. But in times of decadence, the scale of values is reversed, and frivolities, then, appear as great things. And when such reversal takes place, the social edifice not being able to hold out solely on props of technique, sceience and reason must collapse, because the soul alone allows humanity to soar. When the soul makes default, it is the fall and the decadence, for all that loses its ascending force, could not but descend, pulled down by an irresistible force.

When a society reaches this point in its evolution, when the breath that gave it the first impulsion ceases to animate it, it is the end of a cycle and the exodus of the civilization towards another space, where another cycle commences on a new bio-historical synthesis. But in the space, thus becoming vacant, the work of science loses all significance. Wherever there ceases the radiation of the soul, the rational work also comes to a stop. One would say that the man loses the thirst to understand and the will to act, the moment he loses the élan, the "tension of the faith". Reason disappears because its works perish in a milieu that could no longer understand or utilise them. Thus the work of Ibn Khaldûn seems to have come too soon or too late: it could no longer impress itself on the Muslim genius that had already lost its plasticity, its aptitude to progress and to renew itself. And the Qur'ânic impulsion being deadened, little by little the Muslim world came to a stop like a motor that had consumed its last litre of petrol.

No temporal substitute, in the course of history, could replace this unique source of human energy, that is, the faith. Neither the "Tîmûrid renaissance", that flourished in the fourteenth century around the mausoleums of Samarqand, nor the Ottoman empire would give a "movement" to the Muslim world that no longer possessed its resource within itself. The internal contradictions were going to reach their culminating point in

*Cairo was founded toward 960 A.D. by the Fâṭimids.

their inevitable end: the dislocation of a world and the advent of a new society endowed with new characteristics and new tendencies. It was then, the phase of decadence: man, soil and time were no longer the factors of civilization, but inert objects without creative intercourse with one another.

It would be proper here to dispel an ambiguity: one could note that faith never lost its sway in the Muslim world even in this period of decadence—and this remark would become essential if it had concerned an eschatological appraisal of spiritual values. But, if we wish to consider the problem from an historical and sociological point of view, it would be convenient not to confound the salvation of the individual soul with the evolution of societies. The social role of religion is here essentially that of a catalyser, favouring the transformation of values that pass from a natural to a psycho-temporal state, corresponding to a certain stage of civilization. This transformation turns the biological man into a sociological entity; time—simple chronological duration evaluated in "hours that pass"—into sociological time, evaluated in hours of labour; and soil—yielding unilaterally and unconditionally the nourishment for man according to a simple process of consumption—into a technically equipped and conditioned terrain for catering to the multiple needs of social life according to the conditions of a process of production.

Religion is then the catalyser of social values, but in its nascent, dynamic and expansive state, when it expresses a collective thought. The moment faith becomes centripetal and without radiation, that is to say, individualistic, its historical mission on earth comes to an end, where it is no longer fit to promote a civilization. It thus becomes the faith of the devotees who withdraw themselves from life, fleeing from their duties and responsibilities like all those who, since Ibn Khaldûn, have taken refuge in marabutism."[2]

History commences with the integral man, constantly adapting his effort to his ideal and needs, and accomplishing in society his double mission of actor and witness. But history ends with the disintegrated man, the corpuscle deprived of the centre of gravitation, the individual living in a dissolved society that no longer furnishes his existence with either moral or material base. It is then the escape into marabutism, or no matter what other Nirvana, that are but the subjective form of the social escapism.

2. THE POST AL-MUWAḤḤID MAN

"Ah, The misfortune! The times are near when man will no longer throw beyond men the arrow of his desire; when the strings of his bow will no longer know how to vibrate..."

NIETZCHE

While analysing the activities and tastes of the individuals of a given milieu, one comes across certain dominant common traits that are transmitted from one generation to the other; for there is a sociological heredity just like the biological. One could easily perceive it in England where there exists a will for conservation, a "conservatism". It could be seen even more clearly during the entire period of the decadence of the Muslim world when all social forms became static. But these two aspects of heredity are not identical: in the one case, it is a question of aptitude; in the other of inaptitude. The Englishman voluntarily inclines towards a certain traditionalism, judged necessary for national equilibrium; but this equilibrium is dynamic. In the Muslim society, on the contrary, it bespeaks of an impotence to surpass that which is given, to go beyond the known, to cross new historical frontiers, to create and assimilate anew. Here it is no more a question of a determination but of an insolvency.

In one case as in the other, the thoughts and notions of the individuals work themselves out according to the original canvases that are hereditary. One should observe a child at play to understand the importance of sociological heredity and its controlling force. All the traditions of a society are found in the game of a child that constitutes the most elementary and spontaneous form of human activity: one could ascertain that it possesses the same characteristics wheresoever the social life has, for centuries, espoused the same aesthetical, ethical and technical forms.

Similarly, for studying the activities of a country, one must relate them to the condition of civilization where life has adopted the same forms, and the individual has incessantly modelled his thoughts and actions on the same canvas for centuries. It is not without reason that a "serpent-charmer" could charm the children of Samarqand as much as those of Marrakesh. That means the Muslim problem is "one"—not in its variants of political, or even, ethnic, order—but in the essential social order. This consideration authorises or rather obliges us to date this problem in such a way as to place it in history. Consequently it is not a peculiarity of language, but a dialectical necessity, to say that the Muslim world does not live in 1949 but in 1369

One is compelled to underline this date because it forms the point of departure of a "historical process" to which are traceable all the particularities of the Muslim world and the variants that one designates as the "Algerian problem" or the "Indonesian problem". The common denominator of all these problems is, in fact, the Muslim problem and its historical sequence since the *Hijrah*. Now, if one were to depict the processes of this sequence by a curve, one would find the point of inflexion—that marked the reversion of Muslim values into non-values—somewhere towards the epoch of Ibn Khaldûn.

This reversion was not, however, instantaneous; it marked the distant culmination of the Ṣiffīn rupture that had substituted dynastic power for democratic khalīfal power, thus causing breach between the State and the popular consciousness.* This separation in itself contained the potential for all the future separatisms and political antitheses in the bosom of Islam.

Viewed from a purely political angle, this first schism constituted one of the "crises" that in the course of history change the institutional framework of a country. But a moment arrives when there is no longer any person to guard or seize power and to adapt it to new institutions. Then the sceptre itself falls, broken into a thousand pieces, to be picked up by a thousand petty princes.

This moment marks a point of inflexion in the historical evolution, the reversal of the values of a civilization. It is no longer the question of a change in the political framework: it is the man himself, the civilised man, who loses his "civilizing élan": and is thus unable to assimilate and create. It is no longer a question of institutions but of the human factor: these are the men themselves who no longer know how to apply their

* The advent of the democratic spirit which the Najib revolution is sowing in the Muslim countries marks, in fact, the advent of a new popular consciousness that would, more and more, claim the right to supervise the affairs of the State.

genius to their soil and time. It is the fundamental synthesis itself that disintegrates and with it the social life that gives place to the vegetative life. In Muslim history such a phenomenon could be dated from the fall of the al-Muwaḥḥid dynasty,[3] that was the fall of a civilization at the end of its breath. The era of decadence commenced with the *post-al-Muwaḥḥid man.* Even in the days of Ibn Khaldûn, Qayruwân that had known the splendours of the Aghlabid kingdom[4] and had been the metropolis of a million inhabitants, was no more than an insignificant township; on the other extremity of the Muslim world, Baghdâd and Samarqand had suffered the same fate. Everywhere the same symptoms of a general collapse marked the point of inflexion of the curve.

From a sociological point of view, the symptoms that could be discerned in urban or political affairs were but the expression of a nearly pathological state of the new man—the post-al-Muwaḥḥid man who had succeeded the man of Muslim civilization, and who carried in himself the germs whence would sprout, in succession and sporadically, all the problems since faced by the Muslim world. The present lacunae of the renaissance are imputable to this man who is not only the predecessor to whom we owe our sociological heredity and the traditional canvas of our social activity, but who is also our contemporary. He is not only the invisible instigator of our present failures, he is also thereof the co-actor; he has not merely transmitted his psychology born of a moral, social, philosophical and political bankruptcy: he has transmitted himself. One encounters this haunting figure of our past, not only under the amiable and innocent aspect of a *fallâḥ*, or the austere, generous aspect of a nomad, but also under the deceptive aspect of the son of a millionaire, of a diploma-holder, who has apparently acquired all the etiquettes of modern life. His diploma or the wealth of his father gives him, at times, the aspect of a "new man", but if one scrutinises his manners, sentiments and thoughts, one would easily perceive that he is none other than the "post-al-Muwaḥḥid man". Until Muslim society liquidates this passive inheritance of its six hundred years' bankruptcy, and renovates the man conforming to the true Islamic tradition and the Cartesian experience, it would vainly search for the equilibirum necessary for a new synthesis of its history.

Thus one stands today in far greater need of moral, social and psychological sciences than of material sciences. The latter constitute rather a danger in a society where men remain ignorant of themselves. But it is evidently more difficult to know and make the man of a civilization than to manufacture a motor or to teach a monkey to carry a tie.

Generally speaking, under whatever aspect he exists—*pâshâ*, false *'âlim*, false intellectual, or beggar--the post-al-Muwaḥḥid man is an essential component of all the problems of the Muslim world ever since the decline of its civilization, and must not be overlooked in a study envisaging the genesis and solution of problems which are more and more agitating Muslim consciousness. It will be at least necessary that the activities that testify to the awakening of a Muslim consciousness in different sectors of social life, respond to a doctrine of the negative factors, of the causes of inefficiency. Even if he is not always as easy to recognise as under the trait of an Āghâ Khân, the post-al-Muwaḥḥid man is, nevertheless, the incarnation of the *colonisibility*, the typical visage of the colonial era, the clown whom the coloniser makes perform the role of the *indigène* and who could accept all the roles, even that of the "emperor", if the situation so demands.

3. THE FIRST EUROPE—ISLAM CONTACT

"Verily, we created you of a male and female, and made you into nations and tribes, so that ye may know each other".

QUR'AN (49:13)

Since time immemorial, the European has sought his nourishment from the soil. This vital necessity helped him to develop the bases of an agrarian, or as a French sociologist puts it, of a "civilisation de l'herbage". The original synthesis of man and soil having been realised at an early stage, the latter found himself disciplined in terms of very close neighbourly relations that created the notion of property, strictly delimiting it as the fixed space of a human life, of a hearth and a family. Internally this space of life, this "vital space" is essentially conditioned by regular seasonal activities that engender a very precise notion, that of the daily work. The social notion of time, in its turn, incorporated itself in the original synthesis. The climate would lead man to adopt fire as an essential element of his life, and to furnish his interior in terms of his daily work, climate and fire. The table and chairs became the conditions of a very intimate family life wherein the individuals gathered at fixed hours for the common meal.

Externally, this family space necessarily articulated on neighbouring spaces similarly conditioned. The church spirit born of these local agglomerations would little by little give birth to communal life, thus realising the integration of the individuals to an order responding to the conditions and aspirations of a static life.

Neither Roman imperialism, nor Germanic nomadism succeeded, in the course of centuries, in modifying this original canvas of European life. Christianism and Cartesianism came to complete the physiognomy of this society, profoundly, perhaps excessively, penetrated with the sense of utility. The former brought to it the sense of the universal, and through it the dynamism that its static temperament lacked; the latter tailored its fundamental activities for efficiently integrating them in the industrial vitality that was going to surge from its evolution. In this society of centripetal virtues that practised mutual aid, but did not know hospitability, Christianism also deposited the ferment of moral expansionism that would serve as a justification for the Crusades and the colonial enterprise.

The Crusades offered the European civilization an opportunity to turn towards the exterior, and to reap a profitable harvest in the Muslim civilization. The same tendencies pushed it to the discovery of America, and one could here discern the beginning of a profound rupture between a dominating Europe and the rest of humanity, that explains the politics of the world for the last four centuries as well as its present disequilibrium. Howsoever it may be, it was this society marked with the genius of the soil, but where the possibilities of inter-human relationships were almost completely stifled that, towards the 18th century, discovered the Muslim world.

In this world, the individual did not originally seek his nourishment from the soil—which could not furnish it—but obtained it from the beast. He was a shepherd, a nomad or a warrior. The space of his life, his vital space, was as indefinite as the zone—the nearest to his habitat—where the last rain had fallen. This habitation itself was mobile by necessity and could dispense with furniture.

Why settle on a soil that did not give food? The man thus on the move, did not have regular activities, and though he well knew the effort, at times exhausting, that his profession of shepherd and warrior demanded, he had no idea at all of an organized, daily work, which only the soil teaches to those who work on it during the seasons. Content with the warmth of the sun, he did not adopt fire as an accessory of his life. Moreover, this errant life did not impose relations of orderly neighbourhood since the individual did not own landed property. As his nurture did not depend on such relations, his gregarious instinct was little developed, and he did not seek to integrate himself to a social order. The tribe of which he formed a part, was not an order determined by social reasons but rather by biological causes. The relations of the individual outside the tribe, that is, his properly social relations were non-existent.

A world divided in the extreme and atomised into individuals, a world of centrifugal virtues that did not know mutual aid—just as it ignored the efficacy of the matter—but practised hospitality, honoured generosity, and loved vanity, poetry and the horse. Its dynamism explains the extreme rapidity of Islamic expansion, the cause of which the historians have vainly sought in the external conditions. On this canvas Islam came to embroider its admirable civilization, giving to a world dominated by individualism a cohesion and a sense of the collective that determined its historical orientation. The Qur'ân transformed the Beduin into a sedentary, who left in Spain and the south of France, the evidence of a perfect agricultural science.* This fixation of the man to the soil immediately produced its effect: science and art appeared and developed in a disciplined society where the individual no longer obeyed his vagrant humour but submitted to an order and to the laws.

In the 18th century, this civilization had long finished the cycle of its civilization, and the individual found himself once again in the conditions of life offered by an atomised society of abolished activities, save for certain enclaves such as Fez, Qayruwân and Damascus, prestigious vestiges that alone bore witness to a finished past since in general the post-al-Muwaḥḥid man preferred a return to the nomadic life of his ancestors to a sedentary life. Just as a European engineer or artist once seeing the cycle of his civilization nearing its end, would again become a cultivator or a gardener, the Muslim world had reverted to a tribal, nomadic state when the West made its discovery, more than a century ago.

It would be convenient not to forget that Europe which looked upon itself as the sole depositary of the human destinies had already, since the age of Boccaccio—even while its cradling civilisation still drew its first nourishment from the Arabs—disowned purely and simply the Arab civilisation. On this point, it would be doubtless more fitting to quote a European himself. Here are, for example the melancholy reflections of D. Gustave Lebon that conclude his study on the *Arab Civilisation:*

> The reader would ask himself why under these conditions, the influence of the Arabs is so ignored today by the scholars whose spirit would seem to place them above all religious prejudices.... In reality, this independence of opinion is much more apparent than real and we are by no means free to think as we wish on certain subjects. The hereditary prejudices that we profess against Islam and its disciples have been accumulated over so many centuries, that they have become part of our organism.

The tribunal that still decides litigation in Spain concerning the distribution of irrigation water, called "el tribunal de las agua", dates from the Muslim period.

This text indirectly but clearly illuminates the position of the European civilisation vis-a vis the Muslim, at the debut of the colonial era, position to which corresponded the attitude of this Muslim world towards the "things" and "notions" of Europe which it, in general, covered with a sovereign scorn—pretending as it did, to be the sole depositary of Divine grâce. From these given facts, one could easily imagine the internal contradictions which the modern West was going to introduce in the archaic world of the post-al-Muwaḥḥid man.

TRANSLATOR'S NOTES

1. The Athenian scholar (ca. 460 BC) and the author of *The History of the Pelponnesian War*.

2. From *Murâbiṭ*, the warrior monk of a fortified convent (*ribâṭ*); saint. Bennabi uses the term in a pejorative sense in much the same way as Iqbâl uses the term *pîr* or *zâhid* or *ṣûfî* to denote religious escapism or quackery.

3. Al-Muwaḥḥidûn ruled over North Africa and Spain from A.D. 1130 to 1269.

4. The Aghlabid rule in Tunisia (A.D. 800-900) marked the greatest ascendancy of the Arabs in the Mediterranean.

2

THE RENAISSANCE

2

THE REFORMIST MOVEMENT

"Verily, God will not change the condition of men, till they change what is in themselves."

QUR'AN (13:11)

While implanting himself in the Muslim world towards the beginning of the last century, the European presented of his Christian morality, only certain dispositions of his soul — a beautiful soul if one viewed it from the interior, from the point of the convergence of his centripetal virtues, but which would remain closed and impermeable to the Muslims.

In fact, from the exterior, that is to say, in its actual contacts with the Muslim world, the Christian soul was, above all, that of a coloniser who, before embarking for the Barbary coast, the Indies or the Islands of Java, had heard, in the course of evening family re-unions by the fire-side, of the fabulous Eldorados. In his turn, he had parted in search of Peru, and never was the thirst for gold so violent as after the discovery of the "Colony"

If one views it as a sociologist and not as a moralist, the salutary role of the European in the history of the world since the last two centuries, becomes apparent. However detached he was from the rest of the humanity that he disdained — viewing it only as a sort of stepping stone — the European did, nonetheless, pulled the Muslim world out of the chaos of the occult forces, wherein every society that substitutes for the spirit, its simple function, founders, — shadow deformed by the imagination of the visionaries who have lost, along with their sense of the real, the very genius of the soil. By causing the social order, wherein the post-al-Muwaḥḥid man peaceably vegetated, crack on all sides, the activism of the European would give him a new revelation of his social worth. The man from Europe unknowingly played the role of the dynamite that explodes in a camp of silence and contemplation. The post-al-Muwaḥḥid man, like the Budhist of China and the Brahman of India, felt himsef jolted and finally awoken.

He found himself thus in a new order that was not of his making, and before two imperative necessities. Despite his bankruptcy, he must assure himself of the minimum of dignity that Islam demands of all his adepts, even in the primitive societies of central Africa; and he must assure himself of a vital minimum in an implacable social order that no longer nourished either the plunderer living on the razzias, or the hermit living on public charity, or the son of the family living on familial patrimony all possibilities of vegetating were henceforth abolished. On the moral, as on the social plane, the Muslim was thus obliged to seek a *modus vivendi* compatible with the conditions of a new life. From this obscure groping that grafted itself on a lingering uneasiness that Ibn Taymiyyah had left in the Muslim consciousness a few centuries before, stemmed the historical movements that would give the Muslim world its present physiognomy. These movements issued from two currents; the *Reformist* linked to Muslim consciousness, and the *Modernist*, less profound, more fortuitous, and more particularly connected with the aspirations of a new social category, the issue of the Western school, as would be the Alîgarh University movement in India.

The first of these two currents seems to find its way in the Muslim consciousness somewhat like a course of subterranean water, spouting here and there on the surface, from time to time since the days of Ibn Taymiyyah who was neither an *'âlim* like the *shaykhs*, nor a mystic like Ghazâlî, but a militant crusader for the revival of the Muslim world—both social and spiritual. It was the same current that with Ibn Tûmart had surged into the powerful al-Muwaḥḥad empire in the West, and with Ibn 'Abd al-Wahhâb into the Wahhâbî empire in the East, which would be crushed towards 1820 by Mohammad Ali at the instigation of the Sublime Porte and the Western Powers. But it preserved therein, its doctrinal vigour that allowed it to re-appear once again in 1925 under the temporal form of the present Wahhâbî empire.

But it was particularly after the disappearance of the first Wahhâbî empire in 1820 that this current found a consciousness that would reflect it to the modern Muslim world: Jamâl al-Dîn al-Afghânî who had managed to escape, in his isolated mountains, the degrading stigmas of the post-al-Muwaḥḥid society that turned the individual into a victim or a fawning courtier. To his essential quality of the "natural" man, he brought a unique culture that precisely inaugurated the era of the *homo sapiens* in the modern Muslim world. This culture would attract in its wake the cultured youth of Istanbul, Cairo and Tehran who would furnish the leadership of the Reformist movement. This man whose intellectual capacities Professor Gibb seems to put in doubt[1] dared talk, a century ago, in the decayed post-al-Muwaḥḥid world, of the "social function of the prophets."

Al-Afghânî found himself, by an accident of history, the incorruptible witness and the implacable judge of a society that slowly attained its decomposition, while colonialism installed itself on its soil. It was the sepoy revolt[2] and its bloody ending that seems to have catalysed in the conscience of this man the will to reform his milieu. He saw in this drama the moral and material bankruptcy of the Muslim society, as implied in the failure of the revolt and confirmed, in a way, by the ʿAlîgarh movement that appeared in the wake of these bloody events and, in the eyes of al-Afghânî, took on the character of a betrayal of Islam. He forthwith launched an offensive against antiquated institutions and fatal ideas.

On the first plane he sought to undermine the existing powers in order to realize a political re-composition of the Muslim world, founded on "Islamic fraternity" that was breached at Ṣiffîn and finally destroyed by colonial regimes. On the second plane, he led the struggle against "naturism", the term under which he denounced the materialism that he allegedly detected in the teaching of Aḥmad Khân[3] at ʿAligarh and attributed it to the occult influences of the West. Al-Afghânî's attitude appears reactionary, the more so since the University movement later proved to be an eminent factor of Muslim renaissance in India. However, it supplied the necessary corrective to the future orientation of teaching at ʿAlîgarh, just as a century later, the opposition of Azharite scholars, notably of Rashîd Riḍâ, to the thesis of Ṭâhâ Ḥusayn,* far from proving merely negative, exercised a salutary influence not only on the future orientation of Egyptian culture but also on the writings of Ṭâhâ Ḥusayn himself.

Anyhow, al-Afghânî's impetuous temperament made of him a militant rather than a thinker who would carefully examine problems and work out solutions. His extraordinary culture was only a dialectical, even demagogic, means of revolutionary action that had a psychological and intellectual, rather than political, impact on a still totally apathetic Muslim world. It must needs make the Muslim drama manifest in the Muslim conscience itself. It does not seem that this recall to the Muslim conscience of the drama that it carried within itself formed part of a systematic plan: his quite rare written work, mostly polemics directed against the naturists or against Renan, do not allow any affirmation in this regard. But if he was neither the leader, nor the doctrinaire of modern Reformist movement, he was its initiator, at the same time gathering and transmitting, all along his life of a pilgrim, this anxious inquietude to which one owes the modest efforts of the present renaissance.

---

* *Fî al-shi'r al-Jâhilî* (1926)

Fully conscious of the rottenness of his milieu, al-Afghânî sought to cure it through a suppression of its institutional framework rather than through a reformation of the post-al-Muwaḥḥid man. He might have achieved his objective if such a revolution was accomplished, for every revolution is creative of new values, and, as a result, susceptible of transforming the man. But the lever of this revolution was ill-forged; it could be efficacious only if the sentiment of "Islamic fraternity" was transformed into an act: "the Islamic fraternisation", such as it once had existed in the days of *Anṣârs* and *Muhâjirûn*—the first constitutional act that laid the foundation of early Muslim society.

So, while al-Afghânî had been the promoter of the Reformist movement and remains the legendary hero of the modern epic,* he was not himself a "reformer" in the exact sense of the term. That role was reserved for Shaykh ʿAbduh, an Egyptian Azharite. Immemorially attached to the soil, Egypt has always been a society, that is to say, a milieu where the individual is constantly merged into a collectivity, and endowed thereby with the instinct of social realities; al-Azhar has always furnished dogmatic spirits. Having taken cognizance of the Muslim drama ʿAbduh was obliged to transform it into a social problem, whereas his master with his tribal and empirical spirit had seen it from a political angle.

These original dispositions of the Egyptian Shaykh explain the entire genesis and orientation of the Reformist school. Yet, it appears, that the instinct of the soil—which is the quintessence of social sense—and the Azharite spirit separately suggested their solution, perhaps even due to what Gibb calls "the atomism". ʿAbduh knew that for realising a reform of Muslim Society, one must first of all reform the individual. He found for this concept an important reference in the Qur'ân: "God does not make any change in the condition of a people, till the latter has not previously changed what there is in its soul" (Qur'ân, 13:10). In this verse, that became the watchword of the school, notably in North African ʿIṣlâḥism there is a vigorous statement of the entire social problem which is essentially linked to the soul of the individual. But how to transform this soul? Here the dogmatic spirit of ʿAbduh intervened. He thought, as would think later the Indian Sir Muḥammad Iqbâl, that a reformulation of Muslim theology was indispensible.

* M. Aly al-Hammamy, the distinguished Algerian intellectual, spoke of him in these significant words in a recent biography. "His name, like that of Homer for the cities of Attica, would always be claimed by all the Muslim countries."

But the word "theology" became the fatality of the Reformist movement resulting in a partial deviation and devaluation of certain of its leading principles, such as the "Salafiyah" or a return to the original purity of Islam. For theology touches the problem of the *soul* only in the realm of credo. or dogma. Now the Muslim, even the post-al-Muwaḥḥid Muslim, had never abandoned his credo He had remained a believer or more exactly a devotee; his faith had become inefficacious because it had lost its social radiation, becoming centripetal, individualist: the faith of the individual disintegrated from his social milieu.

Consequently it was not a question of teaching him a faith that he already possessed but of restoring to this faith its efficacy. In a word, it was less a question of "proving" God to him than of "manifesting" Him to his consciousness, filling his soul with it as with a source of energy. Transforming the soul is to make it surpass its ordinary bounds. This task did not lie in the domain of theology, but in that of a mysticism, or more exactly of a science that still has no name, but what may be termed, *the renewal of alliance or union.* In an effort of renaissance, mysticism—that has led to *Marabutic* mystification—could not furnish the necessary basis for Reformist action. The mystic did, in fact, aim only at the spiritual condition of certain souls of the elite, while it was a question of general reform, of providing an internal impulsion to the masses thirsting for a (call of) *sursum corda* ('Lift up your hearts') for vanquishing their own inertia.*

These considerations would not have failed to appear to the Reformist school if it could have achieved a synthesis of its ideas by establishing a link between the dogmatic views of 'Abduh and the political and social views of al-Afghânî. It would have indicated quite another path than that of a simple reformulation of theological principles. Moses, Jesus and Muḥammad were not the theologian constructors of abstract propositions, but essentially the accumulators of this moral energy which they communicated to simple souls.

Theology restored respectability to discussion and exchange of ideas, but at the same time it de-naturalised the Muslim problem by transforming the "Salafite" principle even in the spirit of the reformers. This unconscious transgression substituted for the psychological problem of renaissance, a scholastic problem. For with theology the "social function" of

* Talking of the spiritual disarray of modern Europe, Chesterton judged its present mysticism in these terms: "There was a return to mysticism but without christianism. Mysticism had returned alone and brought along with it seven devils stronger than itself...." This judgement could apply *mutatis mutandis* to the Marabutism of post-al-Muwaḥḥid society.

religion is not posed, as the believing man does not learn anything from a school that teaches him solely the existence of God, and does not, in any case, teach the return to the *Salaf*.

To explain fully the Reformist deviation, one must, perhaps, add to the reasons already enumerated what Gibb calls the "superimposition". It existed in European culture in the epoch of Thomas Acquinas under the form of a purge of Muslim influences. Today the same phenomenon is evident in the traditional Muslim culture in the form of a resistence to Western ideas: the theological work of ʿAbduh is finally apologetic because of the ʿsuperimposition'.

A sum-up of this criticism would risk to show us only the lacunae of the Reformist movement, so that the latter would lose in our eyes, if not its historical value, at least its social value. However, the present Muslim world, with all its realisations and virtualities, is, for a great part—the other being that of the Modernist current that we would examine later on—the work of Shaykh ʿAbduh and his school. Even if the great Egyptian Azharite failed to place the problem exactly in the Muslim conscience, he succeeded in posing it on the intellectual plane, provoking an intellectual ferment not only in Egypt but almost in the entire Muslim world. For theology was, in fact, the first effort of Muslim intelligence to disengage itself from its secular lethargy. One must not underestimate the significance of the appearance of *Risâlat al-Tawḥîd* in a field where nothing had happened since Ibn Khaldûn. For the first time since many centuries, a Muslim brain had fathered a thoughtful work. For the first time discussions broke the silence that had reigned in the old universities of the Muslim world. One of them, al-Azhar, where the debates opened by al-Afghânî and ʿAbduh had come to resound, was to show itself particularly sensitive to the new mood—not in its programmes and methods which, despite certain superficial tentatives, still await their re-statement— but in its spirit. Al-Azhar, that is to say, the intellectual centre of the Muslim world had at last admitted the law of movement and progress and realised that there was no such thing as an immutable perfection, but only a state of perfectible things, even under its imposing domes.

Thus the modern Muslim thought set itself to work in the immense field that the Reformist action had opened before it.*

* The author did not deem it necessary to talk here of the students of Jamâl al-Dîn and Shaykh ʿAbduh who were content merely to extend the movement. Ibn Bâdîs, nevertheless, merits mention, but it would be convenient to refer to the study of M. Ali Hammamy, published in *La Republique Algerienne*, 1949.

However this field, left fallow for centuries, was overrun entirely by parasitic vegetation, and a thorough clean-up was necessary in the spiritual as much, if not more, as in the intellectual domain. To the lacunae inherent in the post al-Muwaḥḥid man, there came to be added the lacunae attaching to the institution. An institution has its life, its history and traditions; in a word, its own inertia that at times defies the will of man. To the atomism, dogmatism and the apologetic tendency—that the Reformist spirit could not spontaneously shake off—were added the blemishes of an institutional order: the *mujâdalah,* literalism, hysterics and poetism peculiar to the post-al-Muwaḥḥid culture. How could one move under the weight of centuries and the burden of traditions that had pell-mell accumulated themselves. For building anew, one needed either a revolutionary spirit like Jamâl al-Dîn, partisan of the "clean slate" or a systematic spirit that would have methodically proceeded towards the necessary ruptures to liberate the institution from its traditional shackles. One must have first of all, made a balance-sheet of these indispensible ruptures by a discrimination of the traditions. The word "tradition" (*taqlîd*) is a magical Arabic word that could cover up all sorts of superstitions and mystifications under the prestigious varnish of Islamism.* ʿBy a methodical confrontation of tradition with Islam, Muslim culture would have been rid of a great number of sacrosanct *taqlîds.* Shaykh ʿAbd-al-Ḥamîd ibn Bâdîs would thus succeed in extirpating the false tradition of "*Marabutism*" from Algeria. But this task of detection could hardly be the work of an isolated individual, and in his time Shaykh ʿAbduh was alone. As a thinker, he had furnished the example of intellectual work to a world unaccustomed to thinking; as the rector of a university, he had given to his institution the movement that made it amenable to new ideas. In addition to the ruptures that he operated in the Islamic culture, he had revealed Western culture to the Muslim world by introducing it in the re-organization of his university and in his written work which thus bore its first reflection. From all these initiatives must need gush forth the intellectual upsurge of renaissance. But while the "Meiji" upsurge oriented Japan towards the sciences, Muslim renaissance would remain confined for a long time to the domain where the natural inclinations of the post-al-Muwaḥḥid man, who cared little for efficiency, and the notions attached to cultural institutions that had since long lost their social objective, helped maintain it.

The reformers—I am talking of the continuers—themselves contributed to maintain this state of affairs. The *mujâdalah* would subsist for a long time in literary debates. One did not look for

* While writing these lines, we never thought that one day, a Glaoui would dare talk of "tradition" in the name of Islam.

verities but for arguments: one did not listen to his interlocutor but flooded him with a verbal deluge. The *mujâdalah* was all the more dangerous since it depended, in general, on a senseless love for words, leading to another lacunae of post al-Muwaḥḥid spirit "*litteralism*". The Arab genius that had created the most beautiful of languages, resembled a sculptor who becomes amorous of the statue that his chisel has created. Unfortunately the passion for words is more dangerous than that for bronze, marbel or stone.

It commences by making one lose the sense of proportion indispensible for all positive constructive effort. The least headline of an Arabic journal is edifying in this regard. Recently, a Tunisian journal announcing the arrival of a leader from abroad, greeted him with five or six laudative epithets— *karîm*, *jalîl*, *za'îm*, etc. It betokened, doubtless, an apologetic bouquet, but Arabic words carry an irresistible attraction for the post-al-Muwaḥḥid spirit. The Arabic language thus divinised could no longer evolve. The adoration of its adepts has rendered intangible a syntax irrevocably reduced to a dozen of forms, and it has become sacrilegious to constitute new forms through adapted prefixes—something that would be in accord with the very spirit of this language.

In the independent Muslim educational institutions, the syllabi and methods of instruction also seem to defy time; the principles have remained the same since the Christian Middle Ages. For all that these principles constitute the mental canvas of action, the activities remain in the periphery and at the rhythm of a world that has gone by. One believes sometimes to have changed an entire world of ideas by certain superficial retouches, such as the introduction of chairs and tables in independent Algerian schools. It was, of course, the first step to take, but it would be naive to stop at that.

In the circumstances, it is not astonishing that modern Arab thought has still not acquired the sense of efficacy. The despotism of words and forms impresses a superficial character on every translation of renaissance. One could witness it at the Congress of Islamic Culture at Tunis where a Shaykh, while making a discourse consecrated to the Traditions on "clemency", spent more than an hour in counting out the chain of narrators. Needless to specify that its content remained finally unperceived while the listeners yawned—with admiration. Here one comes across an important aspect of post-al-Muwaḥḥid psychology: all is still more grave while the orator and the audience are in accord over the inefficacy. So much so that the living verities that had once fashioned the visage of Muslim civilization are henceforth but dead verities, buried under beautiful phrases and a vast erudition.

It seems that the idea remains the same as it has been since the decadence; the famous "well of science" wherein science is swallowed up and loses the sense of its social role. Just any discourse on Commentary could furnish the occasion for ascertaining the inconsequences of our present culture which, subjugated by the verb, does not express a concern for *acting* but the simple pleasure of *talking*.

There is another reason for this orientation that the apologetic tendency has impressed on the intellectual effort. In its pre-occupation with the apology of the past, the culture takes on a character of archeology where the intellectual effort is directed not forward but backwards. This retrograde tendency imprints on the entire teaching a retrospective character, incompatible with the exigencies of the present and the future. There results therefrom, in the ideas a sort of the phenomenon of "hysteresis", of a constant obsession with the past.

Two other lacunae would complete this picture of the deficiencies of the post-al-Muwaḥḥid culture: a puerile "quantitatism" evident even in the element bearing a "polish" of Western culture, and a "poetism" that is the particular apanage of Zaytunian youth of purely maternal culture. Quantitatism consists in estimating efficacy and value in terms of a book by the quantity of paper written. As for poetism, it is the aesthetics or rather the coquettishness of litteralism and the apologetic tendency. It is the means, more or less elegant according to the case, of masking the imperfections and insufficiencies, of gilding the errors and placing before the incompetences the screen of rhetoric.

It is clear that all these lacunae, we have analysed, were not of a nature to favour the efforts of the Reformist school that did not or could not know how to eliminate them, systematically, thus leaving intact the problem of post-al-Muwaḥḥid residues in the Muslim renaissance. Moreover, since the disappearance of its last two great figures, Rashîd Riḍâ in the East, and Ben Bâdîs in North Africa, the movement as a whole, finds itself at a new turning. In Egypt, the fundamental idea of creating a new moral basis for Muslim life finds itself transformed and deepened in a new movement, that of Muslim Brotherhood, which would be treated further on. In North Africa, it has been more and more superseded by a very important institution, that of independent education, that has timely fulfilled the enormous gap of official instruction. On this path the Islâḥist idea more or less subsists. Certain young teachers are animated with a salafite zeal, but some others are already no more than simple functionaries. This instruction has the merit of attacking the mortal defect of the post-al-Muwaḥḥid world—illiteracy. But in the absence of a doctrine on culture, Iṣlâḥism propagates a complacent alphabetism that dreams of transforming the conditions of life by communicating, above all, the taste for "Muslim things" and Arab "belles-lettres".

It appears from this balance-sheet, that the Reformist movement did not know how to transform the Muslim soul or to translate into reality the "social function" of the religion. All the same, it did succeed in breaking the static equilibrium of the post-al-Muwaḥḥid epoch by introducing in the Muslim conscience—partially and on the intellectual plane only—the notion of its secular drama. But there remained the task of posing the problem of culture in its generality if the renaissance were to emerge from its embryonic state.

As already noted, the development that goes under the name of "Muslim civilization" was only an accommodation of doctrinal Islam to the state of facts that followed Ṣiffîn. The Juridical schools were hard put to realise such an accommodation in face of a dynastic—hence extra-Muslim—power that was exclusive and tyrannical. So much so, that it is not the Muslim civilization that is the issue of Islamic doctrine, but on the contrary, the doctrines that have accommodated themselves to an imposed temporal order.

Any attempt for the reconstruction of Muslim culture must begin with the re-establishment of pure doctrine over the *le fait de prince* (political power) that has stemmed from Ṣiffîn. This reconstruction implies a return to Islam, that is to ṣay, in particular the extrication of the Qur'ânic text from its triple matrix of theology, jurisprudence and philosophy.

But the Modernists seek to drag the Muslim world in quite another direction by breaking—sometimes violently as Kamâlism did in Turkey—with a "tradition" that is often no more than a cover for the post-al-Muwaḥḥid myth.

THE MODERNIST MOVEMENT

"Would'nt I have been, moreover, flagrantly inconsistent, if wishing to ameliorate the country, I would have balked before the idea of ameliorating man?"

H. DE BALZAC

Far from bringing its entire soul to the Muslim world, Europe brought there only that much of its civilization as concerned the immediate commodities of the colonist. On the "native"* plane, however, it had brought what one calls the "native school". It is from this very small contribution that the Modernist movement of the Muslim world had to start.

The school, on the plane of Modernism formed a counterpart to the *madrasah*** on the plane of reform. While the madrasah presented a relatively rejuvenated Islamic thought, the school introduced new cultural elements in the Muslim world. The former would operate a rupture with the post-al-Muwaḥḥid past, the latter would establish a contact with Western thought. Envisaging this new fact, Iqbâl would remark that "the most remarkable phenomenon of modern history... is the enormous rapidity with which the world of Islam is spiritually moving towards the West". But was this really the case

It could have been so only if Europe had brought its soul and its civilization to the world of Islam, or the latter would itself have gone to discover it on the spot. It does not seem that many Muslims have gone in search of the West. Instead, Europe came to the East not as the bearer of a civilization but as a coloniser, and the young bourgeois Muslim went to Europe only for getting a university diploma or for satisfying a wholly

---

The word "indigene" is employed here in a pejorative sense as understood by all colonial administrations.

The *madrasah* is exclusively the school of independent Muslim teaching.

superficial curiosity. A Zaytûnian[5] student, who after finishing his Islamic studies asked for a scholarship to complete his education in Europe, was told by the concerned cultural organisation that "for studying the French language one need not go to France." That is how the Muslim milieu envisages the role of a student who is going to the West. It is just a question of studying a language or learning a profession, not of discovering a culture. Only the aspect of immediate utility counts.

But this way of looking at things must not be exclusively imputed to the indifference of the Muslim vis-a-vis the West. The "native" school did not disperse elements of European culture, but only certain rudiments susceptible of rendering the "native" fit for European economy. There was no question of detecting and stimulating intelligences but of forming *auxiliaries*, of a capacity at once sufficient and limited.

Despite all this, the conscious being—student or simply a governed, even when treated as an "object" did, nevertheless remain a "subject". And it is as a "subject" that the Muslim judges the European order that he sees around him or squeezes from his insufficient readings. His ideas on European "civilization" must need flow from this rudimentary judgement and from the superficial contact—administrative or commercial—that he has had with it.

On the other hand, the little Musalman who goes to the native school, is the brother of the one who goes to the madrasah. Consequently, the same mental habits, the same sociological heredity that marked the Reformist movement have come to mark also the Modernist movement,—intermingled with the new elements, bookish or empirical borrowings from European life as viewed from the exterior.

For centuries the Muslim spirit has been incapable of delving beneath the surface of the phenomena; the Muslim no longer understood but only learnt the Qur'ân. Now, having judged *grosso modo* the utility of European products, he was not going to criticise them! He did not bother himself to find out how they were created but how they could be acquired. Thus the first stage of modernisation of the Muslim world that would adopt the forms without their content, took shape. This disposition would inaugurate an *entropic evolution* that did not accumulate its means but solely its needs. And the infatuation for the things "modern" went to absurd length in all social classes, among both men and women. One could see towards 1925, during the years of prosperity, motor cars parked under the tents where the fowls were kept. The ceramic wash-basin made its appearance in bourgeois homes where it adorned the "modern" bed-rooms. A significant clumsiness, obviously inspired by the hotel style, that is to say, by a way of looking at the European from the exterior. The woman also partook in this euphoria. Instead of acquiring the art and the taste for a 'bit of frippery', she was content to buy it, according to her condition, from needle-work parlours or ready-made garments stores run by shrewd and gracious European saleswomen. Apparent evolution, that often masks a simple transformation of post-al-Muwaḥḥid content from an archaic to a modern form. This tendency seems to develop in Muslim society as the elite, the offspring of Western school, grows more numerous at the top.

This elite has gradually passed beyond the stage of native school: a certain number of young intellectuals have now spent a term in the Western universities. Naturally, it is in this new stage that the Modernist movement approaches its perfection—if this expression could possibly be used—and its moral and social content becomes quite significant.

Because of the psychology of his maternal post-al-Muwaḥḥid milieu where one passes from the sacred to the profane without stopping at the sublime, from Islamic *ʿilm* to modern education without pausing at the notion of culture, the Muslim student starts with blinkers that prevent him from contemplating the civilization otherwise than from an abstract or futile side in accordance with his disposition for the serious. He generally registers himself in the university of a capital. The Quartiers Latin are the same everywhere: one finds there the bookish and controversial or the superficial aspect of culture, its distractions and its pleasures. From one side as from the other, he can see only the culmination and not the evolution of a society. He does not see the woman who is picking a wild flower, but the one who colours her nails and hair and sits smoking on the cafe terraces. He does not see the artist or the artisan bending over his work to translate an idea into matter. Oriented, from the start, with the sense of utility, he does not remark the energies, obscure but creative—and creative, above all, of moral and social values that render a civilized man superior to the primitive man: culture commences when the intellectual effort goes beyond the objective of individual need. Nor would he have the chance to seize the generous aspect of the civilization, that which nourishes the affectivity of the civilised man and gives the creative impulsion to his genius—so true it is that "the great thoughts come from the heart". Descendant of a world that has sold its relics and manuscripts to the American tourist, he would not discern, besides, the healthy cult of the "old thing" that links the past with the future. He will not see the child learning the sense and respect of life as he caresses a cat or cultivates a flower, nor the labourer stopping at the edge of a furrow for judging his work, in communion with the soil which is the embryo of the synthesis of every civilisation. He would not draw, any more, the lesson of certain follies as that of Bernard Palissy burning his last piece of furniture and his floor for obtaining the enamel.

His unconscious materialism and obsession with the "utile" would not let him see, either, the horrible aspect of this civilization that holds in bondage men whom the machine commands, exhausts and wears out and transforms into "robots of human flesh". He will not see the woman forced to leave her hearth to gain laboriously a loaf of bread in a debasing atmosphere that masculinises women and emasculates men. He will not see this odious side that makes even the degraded post-al-Muwaḥḥid society appear in certain respects frequently superior to a civilization that has lost the sense of the human.

Generally speaking the Muslim student has not *experienced* Europe, but has been content to *read* it, that is to say, to learn rather than to understand. He thus remains ignorant of the history of its civilization; he cannot know how it was formed and how it is in the process of disintegrating itself– by its internal contradictions and its incompatibility with the laws of human order, and because its culture is no longer that of a civilization but has been transformed by colonialism and racism into the "culture of the empire". Even if sometimes guided by curiosity he sets out in search of reality, he finds himself in contact only with the twentieth century Europe, shorn of its secular tradition, nickled, chromited and polished; the modern Europe and the practical materialism of its bourgeoisie and the dialectical materialism of its labouring class. And the intellectual who has not even acquired sufficiently the sense of real efficacy at the European school, by which a Christian still distinguishes himself from a Muslim, would more readily borrow from the materialism of Europe its bourgeois tendency—that is to say, the materialist tastes, rather than its proletarian tendency—that is to say, a dialectical discipline. Having never considered the ontological liaison of European "products" with the natural framework of Europe, he would not care to bother if these tastes had any relation with Muslim life, thus encumbering the latter with a thousand borrowings that possess no raison d'être whatsoever.

This disposition for accumulating indiscriminate borrowings denounces the rudimentary aspect of the Modernist movement.. Civilization is not an accumulation but a construction, an architecture. Concentrating only on its products, one overlooked the structure of Western society, and did not seize its positive symbol at the level of its virtues, incarnated equally by the artisan, the scholar or a simple labourer, but of its temporary signs such as the aeroplane and the bank. One does not see them any more clearly in the structure of the Muslim world, being content in the one case as in the other, to regard what appears the most easily.

It is not astonishing in these circumstances, that the words themselves have been drained of all the contents that form their social value. Certainly the "parole is divine", but only so far as it is an act and not a simple collection of words as happens during election campaings. For exercising its seduction, this litteralism has at its command an entirely new terminology, favourably received in a society, under strain of an effort of recovery. The parole here betrays its mission: instead of directing this "effort" in the direction of *over-effort* necessary for confronting the tasks of the present, it degrades it to an *under-effort* into gestures barely sufficient for securing a seat or an honourable position. The man who pretends to direct public life does not conceive things for *doing* them but only for *saying* them, and talking about them eloquently. This word is purely a verbal act without social potential or moral "tension".*

However, it is this moral tension that essentially characterises all efficacious intellectual, moral and physical attitudes. It is the man in his plenitude who "strains" himself, goes beyond his nature because he constantly modifies it. In such a case, his word is a will, an act that expresses a just relationship between words and realities. But when this relation between word and the act makes default, the former is no more than mere talk. If the liaison between the word—as an expression of thought—and the act—as its concretisation—does not exist in our spirit, we would no more seize the reverse relationship of act to thought, and will miss this perpetual dialectic that goes from new conquests to new words and by these words to still new conquests.

If with the Reformists (particularly since the disappearance of its last great representatives) the word is not founded on a social imperative, with the Modernists it does not aim at efficiency or implicate the practical tension of words towards acts. The common cause of the error of the two movements is that neither went to the very source of its inspiration. The Reformists have not in reality gone back to the origins of Islamic thought, any more than the Modernists to the origins of Western thought. However, on the psychological plane, a discrimination between the two is altogether indispensible. The "Salafist" individually carries the notion of renaissance. Even if

* The term "tension" is used by Gibb, and corresponds to the Qur'anic notion that one could discover in the verse relating to John, the Baptist! "Hold the Book with force... " (Qur'ân: 19:11)

he does not methodically realize therefrom the practical conditions, he at least does not lose sight of the essential objective. He has enough awareness of his milieu to demand only the "duties", leaving "rights" for the Modernist. In peforming his work, however naive, he reaches an understanding of his milieu through his own "reformist" effort. With the Modernist, on the contrary, the very notion of renaissance makes default or is relegated to a secondary position. The Modernist engages himself in the life of his country only on the political plane. For him the primary question is not the regeneration of the Muslim world, but of pulling it out of its present embarrassment. It is a borrowed notion that does not, in fact, envisage the Muslim problem of the man, but the European problem of the institution. This results sometimes in distressing scenes. I have seen in the streets of Algiers, a young man bending over a dust-bin in search of his pittance, while a wall-poster a little above his head, invited him to demand a "Sovereign Constituent Assembly". It well seems that the inspirers of this sinister inconsistency had never regarded from near the man of the people, for seeking to know exactly what would have really and immediately referred to his sad fate.

The modernist movement does not in fact reflect any precise doctrine: it is as indefinite in its means as in its ends. Its only precise path is that which leads the *Musulman* to be a client or imitator without originality, of an alien civilization that more readily opens the doors of its shops than of its schools, where the students could perhaps learn to utilize their personal genius for their own benefit. It would suffice, in this regard, to consider the very composition of the student missions that Egypt annually sends to European universities. One of the most recent (1947) was composed of some sixty students, none of whom was destined for technical studies, and of whom the majority was, besides, Copt. This example, like so many others, shows that the Modernist movement is not oriented towards acts and means but towards fashions, tastes, and wants.* When its

* These tendencies of the modern Muslim world are naturally reflected in its economic life and commercial relations, as may easily be seen from a scrutiny of any international economic review. Here are two indicators taken from the November 1949 issue of *Boom* (digest of Commerce):
Israel
Supply: Cement, marble, asbestos, suit-cases, etc.
Demand: Iron for industry and building, chemical and pharmaceutical products, cork etc.
Arabia (Irâq, Jordan, Kuwayt etc.):
Supply: nil
Demand: Jewellery, hosiery, cosmetic, perfumes, toys, confectionary, preserved fruit, satin, silk, cotton, rayon etc.

representatives attribute to colonialism their own inefficiency, it seems that it is for them chiefly the question of an alibi and that they wish to run away from their true responsibility. This subterfuge is also employed by the Reformist movement which instead of seeking the internal causes of its insufficiencies, contents itself to impute them to foreign political powers. Neither the one nor the other cares to remedy its own shortcomings, but only to mask them from the eyes of the people.*

However, a certain spirit of initiative—sole criterion of the efficacy of the individual has begun to manifest itself in certain intellectual circles, notably in Algeria. In Constantine, for example, a number of doctors have arranged to observe a weekly social day to attend to the poor--an instance of the intellectual seeking to enter the life of his people otherwise than through the customary threshold of elections. The intellectual and the political effort could thus resume normal significance of being the means and not the end.

This does not mean, however, that the political effort of the Modernist movement has always been in vain. It has succeeded in the crystallisation of a collective consciousness that—as we have seen—has been missing in the Muslim countries since Ṣiffīn, and has constituted in these countries a sign-post which designates, if not the essential objective, at least certain, more or less, practical ends capable of drawing the masses from their indifference and apathy. On the intellectual plane, if the movement has not brought—for lack of a real contact with modern civilization and an effective rupture with the post-al-Muwaḥḥid past—the elements of a culture, it has, nevertheless, given birth through its borrowings from the West, to a current of ideas which though debatable have nonetheless the merit of bringing into question all the traditional criteria.

---

* Of Course the revolution has followed its course since these lines were written, that is to say, since the last four years. A new orientation is evident in the Muslim world particularly Egypt, where a ministry of "Orientation" has been created (1954).

TRANSLATOR'S NOTES

1. Bennabi is referring to Gibb's criticism of Iqbal's estimate of al-Afghani. Gibb, op. cit., pp. 28–29.

2. The Indo-Pakistan war of Independence 1857.

3. Bannabi wrongly calls him "Ali Khan",—perhaps a printing error or the result of scanty and ill-informed literature on the Indo-Pak Muslim movement available in French.

4. Bannabi has taken the quotation from Gibb (op. cit., p. 78) who does not give the following lines which accord precisely with the former's critical comments; "... There is nothing wrong in this movement, for European culture, on its intellectual side, is only a further development of some of the most important phases of the culture of Islam. Our only fear is that the dazzling aspect of European culture may arrest our movement, and we may fail to reach the true inwardness of that culture..." Iqbal, op. cit., p. 7

5. From Zaytûna, the old centre of Islamic learning in Tunisia, now incorporated in the University of Tunisia. The Jâmî' al-Zaytûna was built under the Aghlabids in 864 A.D.

ASMA RASHID

3

THE CHAOS OF THE MODERN MUSLIM WORLD

3

THE INTERNAL FACTORS

"Go to, let us go down and there confound their language"
Genesis (11:17)

Hitherto, we have discussed the phenomena from an abstract point of view, that of analysis. We are now going to consider them from an opposite angle: in their life, movement and action. Life does not analyse; it integrates. When the elements available are compatible and assimilable, it makes a synthesis of them; if they are heteroclite and disparate, it makes of them a syncretism, an accumulation, a chaos.

Today the Muslim world is a mixed product of the inherited residues of the post-al-Muwaḥḥid epoch, and the new cultural deposits of the Reformist and Modernist currents. As seen above, this product is not the result of a reflected orientation or scientific planification,* but it is a motley composition of crude archaisms and non-filtered innovations. This syncretism of elements from different periods and different cultures, without any natural or dialectical link, has engendered a world with its head in 1949 and feet in 1369, and that carries in its intestines all the intermediary epochs.

A heteroclite world afflicted with such incompatibilities and contradictions that even a great spirit like Iqbal was assailed by uncertainty over the problem of women as expressed in this melancholy couplet:

> "I too at the oppression of women am most sorrowful. But the problem is intricate, no solution do I find possible."

---

* Such a planification would be indispensable even, and above all, in the domain of culture. There is, however, good reason to maintain a radical distinction between the culture that has for object man and society, and the "kultur" that has for its object the state. The confusion on this point moreover could not be possible without contempt for the every essence of padagogic enterprise.

Iqbal could neither bear her present plight, nor approve the deplorable condition of her European counterpart.* His anguish is a reflection of the general trouble that reigns in Muslim spirit after half a century of reform and attempted adaptation. The current aspect of Muslim renaissance is marked, above all, by the fact that it has adopted "objects" and "needs" in place of "notions" and "means". Thus, one would find chairs and desks introduced in the *madrasah*, without any change in the centuries old curriculum. The advocates of Arab culture show a paradoxical attitude, desiring certain ends, but not wishing to adopt the means necessary for their achievement. For instance, they have not even decided in the field of modern instruction to return to Arab numerical system, adopted by the West since Gerbert. The common denominator of six centuries of decadence brings round the modernist and the reformist tendencies to the syncretist confusion of borrowed novelties and inherited residue. This chaos of unassimilable elements results in discordant and violent contrasts, such as that presented by the sight of a copiously turbaned gentleman sipping an anisette at a bar counter.

Such gross, simple examples could, however, furnish only a very vague idea of the chaos. In every new-born society that sets to organise itself, there are traditional elements beside those of modern inspiration. The latter, borrowed in general from a society already organised, demand for their proper assimilation an effort of analysis and adaptation that in reality constitutes an effort of creation and synthesis. A precise determination and constant vigilance of the critical spirit is needed to impose upon the necessary borrowings, the indispensable conditions of compatibility, utility and *convenience*. The early Muslim society found itself faced more than once by such problems, and in each instance resolved them in a conscious and happy manner, as in the matter of adopting a mode of the call to prayer. This new "necessity" in the Muslim society already existed in Christian society where the call was made by the sound of bells, and one could simply borrow this means. However, the Prophet and his Companions after reflection opted for an original mode of call: the human voice, thus avoiding the import of bells. Here is an example of a new society that creates its own "means" to responed to this new need. To take another example: the choice of the *minbar* is in all probability, an adaptation of the Christian pulpit. But this adaptation did not take place just simply as a 'newneed', but as a psychological necessity and artistic possibility for Muslim society.

* The position of the author on this point is expressed in his recent study, *Les Conditions de la Renaissance*.

Other usages and "traditions" were similarly admitted in the early Muslim society but only after a deliberate choice between one means and the other, between diverse procedures and conceptions. In these conditions, the borrowing became naturally integrated to Muslim life, since it responded at the same time to its objective and its means. In the scientific field we find Farabi and his school admitting the philosophy of Aristotle into Muslim thought after having Islamised it, just as later on Thomas Aquinas de-Islamised Aristotle for adapting it to the Christian society that, in its turn, was being born and organised. Now, since the last century, Muslim society finds itself once again confronted by the same problem.

The Muslim dilemma concerns, on the one hand, the crucial problem of borrowings from modern civilisation and falls in the bio-historical order, and on the other, constitutes a psychological and dialectical problem, concerning the attitude of the Muslim towards his current life.

As to the first problem, one finds that just as in biology blood transfusion is possible only between similar organic constitutions, the sociological elements that characterise different cultures are not all and always interchangeable. One could ascertain it in 1933 in America, when the temporary introduction of the "dry regime" produced a social trouble as grave as the alcoholism which it sought to remedy. One cannot, however, say that American conscience or psychology were by nature opposed to the "dry regime" or that the jâhilî organism was better predisposed in this regard: the prohibition, nevertheless, succeeded in establishing itself in Muslim countries, thanks to the Qur'ânic imperative that introduced it in the psychology and usages of the jâhiliyyah.

Consequently, new sociological elements could be assimilated only in certain determined conditions provided by an imperative need or a superior imperative. But the Muslim society has failed to take count of these conditions since half a century, making its borrowings without any criteria, or criticism, pushed sometimes by force but mostly by snobbism and bankruptcy of the spirit. The confusion reigning in the intellectual, moral and political domains results from a mélange of decayed ideas, inherited from the past, and borrowed ideas, all the more dangerous because of their displacement from their historical and rational context. For instance the adage "each for himself and God for all", found its necessary antidote in European social organisation, but it could only prove fatal in Muslim society where it replaced the essential social principle of Islam, "each for all and all for each". Sometimes the fatal principle is borrowed from a scientific context acquiring thence a pernicious prestige. Thus the Darwinian principle of the "survival of the fittest" has become an adage of our modern moralists who never doubted that what was true in Zoology could be false in sociology, where "the best" often signifies the "worst". Even in Europe this principle torn from its scientific context had engendered the racist philosophies of Gobineau[1] and Rosenburg. Initially the cause of the concurrence and emulation that favoured the material development of the Western world, it soon transformed the "best" into a rotten man who did not recoil from any means that would ensure his triumph over the "idiots" hampered by their scruples, resulting in veritable gangsterism in this Western society that had erected a zoological principle into a moral principle. It is such ideas, pernicious even for the civilisation that gave them birth, that frequently pass into Muslim renaissance, thus accumulating in a society already encumbered with the residue of its own decadence, the residue of another de-composition. A filteration of dead and deadly ideas constitutes, therefore, the basic task of a veritable renaissance, that must be undertaken consciously and systematically.

The incapacity to think and act characterises also the second aspect of the problem, and may be witnessed in the psychological domain by the absence of a dialectical link between thought and its concrete finalisation. One finds, on analysis the process of an activity in the private or public order wanting in one respect or the other. For example, the Iṣlâḥist thought aims at the reform of man, but one never sees the reformer in the places where the object of his reform is to be found--in the cafés, market places and other public venues where the social evils he wishes to correct are directly in evidence. Likewise the programme of an Iṣlâḥî madrasah does not differ essentially from that of a traditional school and the word "Iṣlâḥ" becomes a simple etiquette that may cover useful activities but is truncated from the doctrinal idea.

Besides this divorce between thought and action, the inertia of the Muslim spirit is also imputable to a confusion between the essence of phenomena and their appearance which has, from the beginning, characterised the modern intellectual movement, The science that it has borrowed from the Western universities is not a means of "being better" but of "appearing better". Its inefficacy in the life of the Muslim world can be judged by its failure to produce any outstanding personality in the realm of human knowledge. Gibb wrongly ascribed this weakness of the Muslim intellectual movement to the natural characteristic of a spirit solely directed towards the "known"; in fact, its organic cause lay in the absence of the "intellectual tension", a weakness peculiar to the post-al-Muwaḥḥid spirit. The Reformists too, like the Modernists, failed to modify essentially the intellectual attitude in this respect. Intelligence is constantly the function of the spirit: when the latter no longer possesses its purity, the former no longer has all its depth. The Iṣlâḥist did impress the soul with a certain dynamism, but the latter has remained sterile for want of a systematic orientation. It is the drama of a movement that wishes to liberate itself from apathy, of the spirit struggling against its incoherence, of the man who has been awakened but does not know what he must do.

This organic impotence is reinforced by moral, social and political paralysis, the former being the gravest since it, in a certain measure, determines the others. From the indisputable verity "Islam is a perfect religion" the post-al-Muwaḥḥid man drew the deadly syllogism: "We are Muslims, therefore we are perfect", that tends to sap all perfectibility in the individual by neutralising in him all concern for attaining perfection. It is a long time since ʻUmar Ibn al-Khaṭṭâb regularly took stock of his conscience and often wept over his faults. One finds to-day reigning among the ruling class the most perfect moral quietitude, and no leader would be seen making his *mea culpa* in public.

So, the Islamic ideal of "life and movement" has foundered in the pride and complacency of a bigot who believes to have realised perfection by performing his five daily prayers, without trying to amend or improve himself. The beings immobilised in their mediocrity and their imperfectible imperfection become, thus, the moral élite of a society where verity gives birth only to nihilism. The difference is essential between verity as a simple theoretical concept enlightening abstract reasoning, and active verity that inspires concrete facts. Verity could even prove disastrous as a sociological principle when it no longer inspires action but paralyses it; when it no more conicides with the motification of change but with the *alibis* of individual and social stagnation. It could then become the origin of a paralytic world which Renan and Father Lammens denounced, saying that Islam is "a religion of stagnation and regression".

Moral paralysis results in intellectual paralysis: when one ceases to perfect himself morally, one also ceases to modify the conditions of his life. Gradually thought finds itself petrified in a world that no more reasons, since its reasoning has no longer a social object. The "taqlîd" or moral conformism implies a renunciation of the intellectual effort, of this "jihâd" that was the essential directive of the Muslim spirit in the great period".* After ʻAbduh, "tajdîd" in the Reformist movement

* One should recall the famous tradition of the Prophet: "He who makes an intellectual effort and does not commit a mistake has a double merit; but he who makes an effort and makes a mistake, has all the same, a merit...."

became basically a literary renewal tied to the rules of a stifling traditionalism and classical themes. On the Reformist side, it has remained tied to classical themes: theology, law, philology, scholastic; and in none of these fields, it has gone beyond the landmarks left by the masters of the Reform. On the Modernist side it seems to have moved further with Tâhâ Husayn. Though the work of this writer could not be termed a doctrine whence new tendencies could emerge, yet its very singularity has led to an agitation of ideas, paving the way for discussion and a movement of thought. However, this movement has remained fragmentary and without articulation, for the Muslim world still lacks academies that would direct its intellectual life and establish mutual contact and dialogue as once existed between the Ghazalian and Averroist schools. Thus it comes about that the work of Ṭâhâ Ḥusayn has barely touched the literary milieus of North Africa, while that of Iqbal does not even find an echo therein. Even in independent Muslim countries, thought has not still acquired its personality, its right to be stated, and its social value as the essential basis and means of action. * In Algeria particularly, the thought is not an action but a motif of decoration, that is to say, something that does not come under the law of formal or practical logic, but rather under that of the post-al-Muwaḥḥid aesthetique.**

The absence of a direct relation between thought and action implies blind, incoherent action and results in a subjective appreciation of facts—in their over-estimation or under-estimation. In the modern Muslim world, it has given birth, on the one hand, to a psychosis of the "easy thing" that leads to blind action, and on the other, to a psychosis of the "impossible thing" that paralyses action. In Algeria the latter is based on three well-known axioms:

—We cannot do anything, because we are ignorant.
—We cannot realise that, because we are poor.
—We cannot undertake this work, because there is the colonialism.

While men of good faith thus explain their incapacity, the charlatans use them for justifying their lucrative enterprise of mystification, under the complacent regard of colonialism. However, the least effort of investigation would reveal that these supposed "verities" are but a cover for certain myths.

---

* The fate of Muslim Brotherhood in Egypt under Farook and of Intellectuals in Iraq and Turkey are sure indications of the place occupied by "thought" in the modern Muslim world.

** Just recently an Algerian journal thanked me for an article, that has permitted him "to embellish his first page...."

We are ignorant — it is a fact, and it stems from colonialism. But what is the role of the existing educated cadres? Do they use their education as elementary and immediate means to fight general illiteracy? One has seen how under German occupation, the Israeli intellectuals, despite strict surveillance, were concerned to use their learning for the benefit of their people. There are very few Muslims, pharmacists, doctors or professers who think — in Algeria and beyond their profession — of popular education. Of course, on the electoral plane, the Muslim elite has not failed to demand an increase in the number of schools. But what is the good of multiplying the schools, so long as one does not 'ameliorate' the teaching? By multiplying the nullity, one can never obtain anything but the nullity. If the educated individual is himself inefficacious, if his education is without social efficacy, the myth of 'ignorance' is a dangerous myth because it masks under the problem of the illiterate man, the more profound problem of the post-al-Muwaḥḥid man, whether ignorant or educated.

Equally dangerous is the myth of poverty. It would suffice to consider the social efficiency of the financial means of the rich Muslim bourgeoisie that ranks even below that of the poor class. Very few rich Muslims would suffer to lower their standard of living to help the intellectual or technical formation of a poor child, or to sustain a work of public utility. This bankruptcy is not particular to the individual, but is also found at the level of so-called cultural organisations that would not give up certain wholly superfluous expenses for the sake of encouraging and aiding culture. It is a course of useless spending. It also seems that in this field the poor have no cause to envy the rich. One can, in fact, ascertain the usage that the "poor" make of their money anywhere. I have had recently (1949) a chance to ascertain it once again in a small town in Constantine where a madrasah, the only work of public utility, balanced itself precariously on a modest budget of six hundred thousand francs. Now an overall, on the spot, survey allowed me to calculate that the "poor"—and they are really so—, had spent in one single evening more than two hundred thousand francs in between two cinemas, a circus, a travelling booth and a number of cafés. Basing on figures of this sort, one could appreciate the *rate of efficiency* of the Muslim capital, that is to say, the relation between the *budget of utilities* — e.g. that of a madrasah — and *the budget of futilities* — such as those of we have just enumerated. In the chosen case, the wastage is 95%. It is an indication of the entropic evolution that reigns in all the fields of modern Muslim life. The wastage ratio mounts even higher during the ceremonies—marriages, circumscisions, funerals, that cause frightful budgetary haemorrhages in the life of Muslim families. The same is the case in public life. In 1948 the U.N. delegation of Arab League in Paris disposed of a 500,000 dollar budget, yet it failed to publish a single document on the Palestine issue, while the Israelis inundated the world with their propaganda. This enormous disproportion between the means and the results is typical of all the Muslim public activity. We are no doubt "poor" but we show no concern in remedying it by a more judicious utilisation of the available means. The case of the Arab League is no exception. In all domains, public or private, wherever money exists, it is ill utilised.* Even if the budget of the Arab delegation had been increased, it would'nt have resulted in an augmentation of their means and efficiency but only of their needs and expenses. For the problem before the Muslim world is not financial but psychological and technical—that of the "orientation of the capital".**

There is finally the third myth which, under the name of colonisation, paralyses all good wills, often justifying veritable moral and political swindlings. It is important to note concerning the myths under discussion that the inhibiting cause does not come from outside but from within, born of the psychology of the men, the ideas, the tastes and usages that constitute the post al-Muwaḥḥid spirit, — in a word, from their "*colonisibility*".

The role of colonialism is certainly crushing, since it strangulates each thought and intellectual effort, each tentative of moral or economic recovery, that is to say all whatsoever that could give an impetus to "native life."*** It technically inferiorises the humanity delivered to its law,—this law that we have designated the "colonising coefficient".**** But this coefficent does not affect the fundamental worth of the individual that escapes his power. Now, we find the individual inefficacious and inert even in domains where the colonial pressure cannot be incriminated. Thus colonialism acts, at the same time, as a reality when it effectively inhibits action,—and as a myth when it becomes an alibi or a mask for colonisibility. There is a historical process which must not be overlooked if we are

---

* One must note the case of Aly El Hammami. His tomb is punctually honoured, but none of the organisations that thus pay their homage have even dreamt to do the only thing that counts; to publish his works.

** See the chapter devoted to this problem in *Les Conditions de la Renaissance*.

*** What could be more significant than the representation made by the French authorities in Morocco to the Americans that the latter must not pay their Moroccan workers wages above a certain rate? The "protector" demanding a decrease in the bread ration of his protégé—but there is all the same something that must have a relation with the "civilising mission...."

**** See *Les Conditions de la Renaissance*.

concerned with the essence of things rather than their appearances. This process does not commence with "colonisation" but with "colonisibility" that provokes it. Moreover, colonisation is to a certain degree the most fortunate effect of the colonisibility because it reverses the social evolution that has engendered the colonisible being: the latter becomes conscious of his colonisibility once he is colonised and thus finds himself obliged to "de-indigènise" himself and become incolonisible. It is in this sense that one can understand colonisation as a "historical necessity". Here a distinction should be made between a country simply conquered and occupied and a colonised country. In the former, a pre-existing synthesis of man, soil and time, implies an incolonisable individual; in the other, the existing social conditions betoken the colonisibility of the individual, and foreign occupation inevitably becomes a colonisation. Rome had not colonised but conquered Greece. England, while it had colonised 400 million Hindus, could not colonise Ireland. On the contrary, Yemen though never colonised, could not profit from its independence because of its colonisibility. Morocco though independent till 1912 did not profit from the experience of Algeria, colonised on its very frontiers since a century. It is from the moment of its own colonisation that it has embarked on a real effort of recovery under the inspiration of Sidi Mohammad ben Youssef.

Thus colonisation is not the primary cause to which one may impute the bankruptcy of men and the listlessness of spirit in Muslim countries. For carrying a valid judgement in this field, one must follow the colonial process from its origin rather than to take count only of the present moment; that is to study it as a sociologist and not as a politician. One would then ascertain that colonisation introduces itself in the life of a colonised people as a contradictory factor that helps it to surmount its colonisibility. By the intermediary of colonisation, colonisibility thus becomes its own negation in the consciousness of the colonised; the latter then forces himself to become non-colonisable. For more than half a century, the history of the Muslim world has merely represented the development of this contradiction introduced by colonialism in the state of things that characterised and constituted colonisibility. There is thus a positive aspect of colonisation in that it liberates potentialities that have for a long time remained dormant. Even if it constitutes, on the other hand, a negative factor since it tends to destroy the very same potentialities by applying to the individual the "colonising co-efficient", one fact is significant: history has never recorded the perenniality of the colonial fact—the essential forces of the man finally surmount all the contradictions. Naturally, coloniser does not come to "promote" but, like a spider, to paralyse its victim; but at the end of the count, it so radically changes the conditions of his life that by its very force, it transforms his soul. Hence, while examining the situation in a colonised country, it is fundamental to consider, turn by turn, these two concurrent yet quite distinct notions—colonisation and colonisibility—and to determine in what measure the cause of inhibitions relate to the one or the other. This is the only way for the Muslim world to arrive at appropriate means for making an end of the deficiencies that have hitherto blocked all its enterprises.

The entire success of a method--whether it concerns a Political doctrine or an Iṣlâḥ — depends, in the first place, on a simultaneous consideration of these two aspects of the problem. Seeing the one without the other is to falsify the problem*.

Unfortunately, this fashion of truncating the problem is, in general disguised under the mask of patriotism, a patriotism loquacious and vain. Is it not, however, the best means of serving colonialism since it helps perpetuate the deficiencies, the paralyses and the abscesses which have already constituted for three or four centuries the obvious signs of a society in a state of pre-colonisation? We are then, forced to the logical and pragmatic conclusion, that, for liberating oneself from an effect: colonisation, one must first get rid of its cause: colonisibility.

Colonialism is responsible for the dearth of the desirable means for developing his talents and material resources, but the unwillingness of the Muslim to utilise the available means, and to exert the required over-effort to raise his standard of life denotes colonisibility. An analysis of the causes of inhibition that hamper the evolution of the Muslim world, would reveal that they are overwhelmingly the result of the internal factors, that is, of colonisibility. This may best be ascertained in the political field which resumes the moral, intellectual and social content of a milieu and of a people, because of its direct relation with life, the one being the planification of the other. For politics is, in its essence, the enterprise of regulating the successive transformations of the condition of men. This relationship, while defining the condition of the individual as an end of all politics, also designates him as an agent in the pursuit of this end, thus doubly implicating him in the political enterprise as both subject

* I would like to offer for the meditation of the reader, this text from Marx which cannot be termed either idealistic or utopian. He addressed it in 1850, in the form of a letter, to those whom he labelled the "alchemists of the revolution": "In place of real conditions, they (the coterie of alchemists) consider desire as the motor of the revolution. We say to the workers: you would go through 15, 20, 50 years of civil and international wars, not only for transforming the conditions (external) but for transforming your own selves and for rendering you apt for political power".

and object. Now the condition of post-al-Muwaḥḥid man is that of a colonised and a colonisible. The relation of subject with object is, here, between the colonised and the colonisible. and not between the colonised and the coloniser. This remark exposes the shallowness of the "politics" in practice in the Muslim world—particularly in North Africa, where it addresses itself exclusively to the coloniser. On the other hand, the colonised is naturally in need of means for acting on the condition of the colonisible, There, again, the politics in question constitutes a heresy since it demands their means of action from the coloniser himself: paradox of a captive who would demand from his jailor the key of his cell.

It is essential to know the given stage of the evolution of a people to determine the politics that would correspond to it. It is a question of the "*stage of civilisation*" and not of "*political status*"--the second aspect being only a certain projection of the first: there are monarchies where one is down at heels and republics where one dies of hunger. One could study the degree or stage of civilisation by observing the manner in which man adapts himself to his milieu. At the stage of vegetative life, man adapts himself by a sort of *under-effort* that involves the least amount of exertion and movement. While, at the stage of active life, he adapts himself by an *over-effort,* that is, by a conscious and technical organisation of his life against cold, hunger and other contingencies. This passage from the vegetative to active life, that marks the commencement or re-birth of a civilisation presents no incomprehensible phenomenon, but comes about through means furnished by the man's own milieu and realised by the most natural powers of man as applied to himself, his soil and his time.

So the colonised man must, despite colonisibility and colonisation, find in his own milieu the fundamental rudimentary means. The soil, time, and his own genius are at his disposal; these original means could be transformed into more perfect means in the measure he transforms himself and becomes conscious of his humanity and the responsibilities that it implies. For being an applied sociology rather than a simple demagoguey, political activity should then imply two postulates:

—to make the politics of its means;

—to procure the means of its politics.

Two successive stages would result therefrom:

(1) A politics compatible with the primordeal means immediately available,—the man, soil and the time. This condition would not exclude, however, the secondary means furnished by chance, or as one calls them today, the conjunctures. But it

must be borne in mind, that the latter do not constitute the fundamental bases of a politics, but just simply its chances, the supplementary possibilities presented by hazard. If one leaves too much room for uncertainties, one would land oneself in a sort of political romanticism.

(2) The progressive transformation of original means into perfect means, capable of modifying in turn the various circumstances of the milieu. This stage would naturally end in the suppression of all forms of colonialism, whether occult as in Yemen, or declared as in North Africa.

The above two principles do not imply a *form* of politics but a *content:* the label could be indifferently, parliamentary or autocratic, but its positive content alone determines if it is applied sociology or a simple mythology. Unfortunately, while following the general evolution of Muslim politics uptil the Palestine affair, one does not have the impression that it rests on well-determined principles and clearly established postulates. Nor could one find real and realistic objectives controlled by a doctrine that would indicate ways of achieving them technically. Even the traditional principle that Jamâl al-Dîn had already formulated by designating "Islamic fraternity" as the basis of all politics in Muslim countries, is continuously combated by diverse nationalisms which are, in fact, only "partyisms", that is to say, the expression of the élites in no way concerned about the relations that they should establish between Muslims, caring only for their own interests. It is difficult to apply the term *politique* to the anarchical initiatives of these different elites, and it would be preferable to apply to them the term "*boulitique*" that the Algerians employ for denoting the confusions, illusions and the myths that masquerade under this label. It exposes the entire difference between chance and sentiment, and a precise direction distilled from human experience in the course of history. The "boulitique" is only the confusion of the possible and impossible, and the abandonment of the accessible and direct means for those inaccessible and imaginary, inevitably leading to the contradictory psychoses of the "impossible thing" and the "easy thing".

This political mythology still masks from Muslim consciousness the true facts of the problem, indulging in mere words when action is needed, denouncing colonialism instead of colonisibility without any effort to transform effectively the condition of men. Even the most serious leaders wait for conjunctures, that is, chance, and in the meanwhile are content to voice their demands by appealing to, no matter what myth: the U.N.O. or the "universal conscience". For the partisans of such an attitude, moreover, the theory of conjunctures is no more than a simple word, a vain hope in face of events that always come to pass unexpectedly. Evidently, one would not know how to discover the sense of the conjecture if one did not possess a sense of reality, stripped of all romanticism and sentimentalism. Unfortunately judgements are most often no more than sentimental professions of faith. One does not judge, but either condemns, hates or loves. Even Sheikh Ben Badis in 1934 merely deplored the "shedding of Muslim blood" in the Arabian peninsula as if he did not discern the grandeur of the conflict wherein the forces of decadence led by Imam Yahya, backed by the colonial powers wrestled with those of the Islamic material and spiritual renaissance incarnated by the Wahhabi thought. This judgement neglected the instructive side of the drama—the rapidity of the manoeuvre of the young Saudi army that foiled the colonial plan in twenty-four hours by taking Hodeiba, and the attitude of Mussolini who would have willingly installed himself in Yemen for "protecting Islam". More recently the Arab press in general dismissed Chikakly's coup-d'état (1949) with regret over the continued instability of the young Syrian republic,* when it betokened in fact the first political move in the country taken independently, and in defiance of the British intelligence.

The most glaring effects of "boulitique" are to be seen in the Palestine debacle. The British knew well what they were doing when they surreptitiously quitted Jaffa, without previous transfer of power to a regular authority organised to protect the entire civil population. Bernard Shaw—but it was generally believed that he spoke only to make a witty remark—said some days before the event, that "the Arabs and Jews should be left alone to settle their differences by arms". It was certainly the opinion of a well-informed man, or of one capable of reflecting before forming an opinion. With the exception of Ibn Saud, all the Arab League members were so stunned that they did not even dream of denouncing the British evacuation which, in the given circumstances, could only benefit the Israelis. Nor did they think of forestalling events by creating a legal situation through the proclamation of a Palestine state. Deceived by the psychosis of the "easy thing", the Arab League counted on U.N. alone, all the while grossly underrating the diplomatic, financial, technical and even the numerical superiority of the Israelis, who could mobilise 300,000 men as against the combined Arab total of 200,000. The Israeli victory was, indeed, easy to foresee for all but the victims of the "boulitique", the latter being neither a science, nor an experience, but a misleading ignorance that goes on repeating its errors.

Thus we find that even when it became evident that the League of Nations was not charged to apply the celebrated

---

* It refers to the three coups d'etat of Zaim, Hannaoni and of Chikakly in 1949.

"fourteen points" of the American statesman but to distribute fresh mandates and protectorates, no practical conclusion was drawn and the game re-commenced with eulogies of the Atlantic Charter and the U.N. as the panacea for all international problems. Pakistan and Indonesia's access to 'easy' independence, that is, independence acquired without great constructive effort, and so to speak, without means, further helped to re-envelop the Muslim consciousness in the enervating vapours of mythology. One failed to see the precarious nature of liberty that did not stem from a liberating principle, but was linked to demands of international strategy liable to change at any moment. One could see it in Indonesia where Queen Wilhelmina changed attitude twice or thrice at the whim of circumstances. Japan must be crushed: the Queen grants independence. Japan is vanquished: the Queen sends an expeditionary force "to cull" the nationalist leaders from their beds and to put an end to the republican euphoria. And when Mao-Tse-Tung finally reaches Canton, the same Queen modifies anew her policy towards Java.*

Examined from close quarters, the situation in Pakistan appears as confused. It seems that Churchill wanted to attain in India three distinct objectives, that is, to deprive the Soviet Union of an effective propaganda weapon, to provide a security zone in Asia against Communism and to create an India-Pakistan antinomy that would, on the one hand, isolate Islam from the Hindu mass, and on the other, prevent the formation of a powerful Indian Union. The irritant of Kashmir was further designed to guard against a reconciliation between two brothers-enemies. Would they understand, in particular, the Machiavellian sense of the declaration made by a Zionist leader: "Relations would have to be established between the state of Israel and the Hindu state for removing from Islam its virulence." In plain language it signifies that the two states that partake the sub-continent must be at war with each other.

It would seem then, that the peoples of North Africa could only liberate themselves from colonialism as a result of similar international circumstance.** But they would not achieve a

* An inquiry on Indonesia published by a Parisian Journal, some months after the editing of these lines, strongly confirms my pointof view. That is how Merry Bromberger sees the new situation in the archipelago: "However", he wrote, "the Dutch present this evening are smiling and agreeable. All is lost *in appearance* (the italics are mine) for them. But all *could be still regained....*" *Paris-Press*, August 30, 1950.

** The French colonialism—as the post-war period demonstrates—does not liberate the colonised peoples but loses the colonies. This even seems to be its vocation, if one looks back on Canada and India. In our days, it is Ho Chi Minh who is liberating Cambodia and Laos.

veritable liberation unless they themselves technically prepared the conditions of their liberation. It would be wrong to assume that the liberation of one country renders "inevitable" the unconditional liberation of another. There are two possible attitudes: wait for the conditions to realise themselves or prepare them in a positive manner.

The capital problem remains: for ceasing to be colonised one must cease to be colonisible, cease to indulge in mythology. While writing these lines, the author still finds the politics of North Africa centred on appeals to U.N. and diatribes against colonialism;* there seems to be no new orientation, no indication of concrete means of definition of daily effort needed to change the factors of colonisibility, and thereby those of colonialism.

The Palestine affair, nevertheless, seems to have somewhat troubled the general euphoria and may well mark the historical turning point leading the Muslim world towards a positive orientation.

---

* See the article in question in the Feb. 3, 1950 issue of *la Republique Algerienne*.

ASMA RASHID

THE EXTERNAL FACTORS

"Verily, when the tyrants enter a city, they pervert it, and humiliate its élite. So do they act."

QUR'AN (27:34)

While the internal aspect of the chaos in the modern Muslim world is attributable to colonisibility, its external aspect relates to colonisation. Here, colonialism not merely manifests itself as an inhibiting myth, but also under the tangible form of eliminating acts which tend to destroy the values of individual and the possibilities of his evolution, as may best be seen in countries under "totalitarian" colonialism as was prevalent lately in Indonesia and Tripoli and exists today in North Africa. The above two aspects interfere and confound with each other, but it is necessary to treat them separately in order to determine their relative importance. One must also define "totalitarian colonialism". Unlike, what may be termed "liberal" colonialism that in appearance at least, leaves a free hand to the colonised, the former intervenes directly in all the domains of the life of the colonised, penetrating even into the details of his religious life. This interference extends to all: One would assign to the children of the colonised a 'native' school that would 'indigenise' his spirit; and if the colonised is a cafe-owner, one would assign to him a social sense that would 'indigenise' his commerce.

This totalitarianism has its academies (Schools of Colonial Sciences) its general plan, and periodical congresses, masking their objectives under various names—Volta Congress, Amis de Nostradamus etc.,—that keep up to date its colonial policies and technical planning of moral and material colonisation.

It is not only through its direct contact between the coloniser and the colonised, that colonialism acts as an essential element in the Muslim chaos, but also, in an occult manner, through rapport of Muslims among themselves. Its "presence" the word is a whole programme manifests itself in the most insignificant details of daily life. One may witness it any day in the streets of Algiers, where a policeman could be seen chasing away a poor boy selling oranges while turning a blind eye to the degrading spectacle of beggar boys spinning out a doleful tale for a few pennies, or a turbaned "soothsayer" grovelling before a foreign tourist. The Quranic verse, "Verily, when the tyrants enter a city, they pervert it and humiliate its élite", illustrates well the colonial philosophy. Colonialism is methodic: all its work is a stage-production, a trick for giving to the country an "indigène" air. All danger that could encounter its work is systematically set aside. It eliminates the veritable élite—not the one its particular favour has designated for representing the people—but the natural elite that testify to the highest virtues of a people. That it may not reform itself, that it may not emerge anew, there is installed a system of perversion, debasement and destruction directed against all dignity, all nobility and all modesty. This technique of disorientation adapts itself continuously to new situations, sabotaging all initiative. The "Muslim renaissance, particularly since Afghani shattered the post-al-Muwahhid equilibrium, could not but excite its most passionate interest, and its unbounded power and ambition has inspired it with the mad and tragic idea of halting the march of civilisation in the colonised country. To counter *tajdīd* it has set up an artificial archaism as a theatre scene wherein its puppets —marabouts, pashas, fake âlems or University degreeholders—must play the scene of the "*Islamic tradition*",—"tradition" that has become the pass-word of the entire colonial policy.

One sees on the other side, the reformist effort countered by a boisterous obscurantism that continuously resucitates dead and buried anachronisms and myths. Since colonialism tries tirelessly to re-edify the ruined pantheon of maraboutism, one would find parading in certain capitals the mummified figurines drawn from the post-al-Muwaḥḥid middle ages to represent the "traditional Islam" in the retrospective scene of native politics. At each instant colonialism shouts at the history of the colonised people the words of Joshua, "stat sol!", "Stop Sun!". This singular pretension which never entered the brain of any Genghis Khan or Attila, is today the political formula of the most odious form of human despotism in this twentieth century of Christian European civilisation.

Guided by the sacrilegious idea of halting the march of the peoples towards light, colonialism has not hesitated to confuse the sacred with the profane. Early in the twentieth century a number of falsified scripts of the Qur'ân were circulated in Egypt in order to sap the very base of Islamic renaissance. When the deception was discovered, those responsible did not scruple to make a joke of the whole thing. The author himself heard an eminent professor in Paris declaring: "Why should the Muslims worry to protect the Qur'ân, since Allah himself has undertaken to safeguard it?" It is indeed difficult to describe all the discordant details introduced ceaselessly in the Muslim life as the grains of sands in the wheels of a motor: the resurrection of maraboutism even when rejected by the people, the choice of morally and physically deformed persons to "represent" Muslims in various assemblies, putting the stamp of "indigène" on the housing projects for Muslims designed to efface the memory of the beautiful Arab style immortalised in the monuments of Spain, the compulsory labelling of native-owned cafes as "cafe maure" where, as in Tunisia, one may be obliged to cater for *kif* smokers so as to make them forget their past, present and future. The colonial work is in fact an immense sabotage of history.

If the world has not been definitely demoralised, and has not lost all moral sense, it is because the human soul is indestructible and eternal, and theologians of all confessions owe thanks to colonialism for demonstrating imperatively the immortality of the soul. No other age has known better to regenerate in the man the attributes of the brute by concoctions of its well-run and well-provided laboratories: laws, banks, administrations, journals and "native" schools. Thanks to them, the dreg of Muslim society has come on top and its élite is at the bottom. Even the intellectual life of a colonised country is a mere ferment for distilling certain ideas that the coloniser carefully culls, for turning them into the guiding ideas of the "boulitique".*

Ever since his primary certificate examination, a child becomes the unconscious object of a conspiracy by the "honourable" examiners who take good care to ensure that a "little native" might not get a more honourable mention than his European comrades. The same applies to the soldier in the ranks. As Marshal Franchet d'Esperey said in the course of a review: "for the native officer, the grade is not a right but a favour". For the little child at school as for the Muslim intellectual the diploma or situation are not rights but favours. One can well conceive, the pitiable samples of Muslim élite that are considered worthy of such favours. On the contrary, if a remarkable intellect appears, one tries to break him by all means and if he proves too hard, one would break his family to paralyse him.

On the economic and social plane, the policy follows the same procedure: to destroy the existing armature and to prevent its reconstitution by all means. Thus one finds Britain in Egypt,

* The same spirit governs today even the "native intellectual life". Subject to colonial literary jureys that give the highest award to the romance wherein the "native genious" has given full measure of its degradation.

effacing the thought of Mohammad Ali and the work of Khedive Ismail who tried to build a national industry in Egypt--not to speak of the 50% shares of Suez wrested from a terrorised government. Similarly, in Algeria social and charitable institutions functioning at the time of French occupation were made to disappear in one way or another. Today, the precious art of miniature painting in the Muslim world has been left with rare representatives, like Omar Racim in Algeria: when these artists will disappear, their art will perish with them, since the administration far from supporting it, has done its best to obliterate it.

So, one finds appearing together in all domains of life, the twin faces of the chaos — colonisibility and colonisation. If the cultural life itself does not escape from the control of colonisation, it is because the latter knows that religion remains the sole and ultimate means of rebuilding the moral health of a people that in the crisis of its history has lost all moral sources. If there is something that vibrates still in Muslim soul, that renders him capable of transforming and surpassing himself, it is Islam. Hence this power of resurrection becomes everywhere the target of attack and an object for all sorts of restrictions and surveillance. It is today infinitely easier in Algeria to open a gambling house or a café than a Quranic school. On the other hand, the administration itself appoints the personnel of the cult, who are chosen not on account of their piety or knowledge but their utility to the administration, thus confronting Muslim conscience with the profoundly disturbing phenomenon of an *imâm* who is an informer, a corrupt and corrupting *muftī* and a prevaricating *qāḍī*. One wishes to make of Islam itself a picturesque aspect of the "native life", thus piling up obstacles and impediments in the path of Muslim renaissance.

But here at least, a direct confrontation becomes possible between colonisibility and colonisation as factors of paralysis, permitting us to realise, very vividly, that the colonised could always rid himself of his colonisibility in the measure he aplies his intelligence to surmount difficulties, avoid pitfalls and to break the shackles. Here at least, for even at the post-al-Muwaḥḥid stage, a Muslim will not suffer attack on his religion,--we see him, notably in Algeria building new mosques and schools, where he can pray freely, and his children could freely pursue their studies. These initiatives have proved to us that it is not a question of discoursing on the liberty of the cult of the extension of education, but of performing social works and accomplishing imperative duties. It is, of course, excellent to obtain the rights that one has demanded but it is not a question of reversing the order of values by putting the 'rights' before the 'duties'— this could only increase the confusion, the disarray and the chaos by multiplying the *faux pas* of the "boulitique".

Colonialism still rings midnight, but in the Muslim world, the hour of sleep and phantoms has irrevocably passed away.

TRANSLATOR'S NOTE

1. Comte de Gobineau (1816–1882) French diplomat & man of letters, and author of the *Essay on the Inequality of Human Races*.

●●●

4

THE CHAOS OF THE WESTERN WORLD

"And they devised and God devised. But of those who devise is God the Best".

QUR'ĀN (3:54)

4

In noting the "enormous rapidity with which the world of Islam was moving towards the West", Iqbal merely referred to a particular aspect of a phenomenon that Ibn Khaldûn had seized in its generality. "The conquered people", the great medieval historian wrote, "adopt the forms, the ideas and the manners of the conquering people." It is this same phenomenon, known as the "law of adaptation" in modern phraseology that confronts today the Muslim world. The anguish and hesitation that, as earlier mentioned, had troubled Iqbal in his quest for a solution to the problem of women, point to the general perplexity of the modern Muslim consciousness before two solutions that appear equally deplorable. It seems that in most cases one is searching for a third solution that would be compatible, at the same time, with the spirit of Islam and the demands of modern age. The hesitation and anguish involved in the search have resulted in a sort of pause in the evolution of ideas, a "historical no man's land", since the Muslim society could neither return to the post-al-Muwaḥḥid stage, nor make a blind thrust forward in its movement "towards the West". For the latter no longer exercises the irresistable fascination and influence it wielded in the epoch of Mustafa Kemal and Iqbal; the West in its turn, represents to-day the spectacle of but another chaos, wherein the Muslim spirit in its search for an "order", does not find a model to imitate or the source of external inspiration that could guide its progressive march. It is thus forced to fall back on its own values, and so one remarks in the writings and discourse of young Muslim intelligentsia a renewed interest in Islam which is, in no sense, a withdrawal. Indeed the Muslim world seems to open itself in a more conscious manner towards the modern world, with the knowledge that though the West could not provide it with all the solutions, as it had fondly believed in the Kemalist epoch, yet one would find therein the results of a highly edifying experience, that constitutes at once the most perfect achievement and the gravest failure of human genius——prodigious lesson of history for understanding the destiny of peoples and civilisations. This double intelligence of events becomes all the more necessary as the Muslim world in its present pause,—since the Palestine affair,—seems to strive at a real comprehension of its problem through a more objective evaluation of the factors of its renaissance as well as those of its chaos.

One has remarked already a tendency to try to grasp the sense of the European historical process, rather than to copy it purely and simply. By seizing the relativity of the European phenomena, one would find it easier to understand their imperfections as well as their real grandeur, and the contacts and exchanges would become more fruitful with this Western world which must, for a long time still, provide the canvas of one's thought and action.

In fact, it is the universal radiation of the Western culture that makes its present chaos a world problem, that has to be understood and analysed in its liaison with the human problem in general, and by consequence, in its liasion with the Muslim problem. Such an analysis could not fail to give the Muslim a chance a placing himself as man, and not as *indigène* with regard to the European order, and to the purely material inter-dependence that at present constitutes the essential relation between a more or less colonial Europe and a more or less colonised Muslim world. Thus, there would succeed a state of mutual esteem and more fruitful association. Such a modification would not be solely beneficial to the Muslim world, for colonialism weighs as heavily on European life: colonialism that materially kills the colonised, also destroys morally the coloniser.

While one could note a tendency among the colonial nations to modify their political relations with the colonised countries, a sort of fatality seems to neutralise this awareness of the colonial peril. The colonial habit seems to be too deeply ingrained in European society to allow the new turn of mind to modify the psychology and the usages that lie at the basis of its moral chaos. It would suffice here to point out the relation of the latter with the chaos in the Muslim world.

The European chaos, like the Muslim, presents a double aspect. The first is merely the simple and ineluctible culmination of a historical movement, while the second is an accidental aspect that results from the incidence of the colonial fact on the life, habits and the ideas, for more than a century. These two aspects merge together in a phenomenon common to all the civilisations: the retardation of consciousness over science and the march of thought. Consciousness is, in fact, the psychological resumé of the history, the distillation of the past in a human "ME", a crystallisation of habits, prejudices and tastes. All acquisitions of thought, therefore, if they have no direct link with the past, the tradition and habits of a people remain beyond the grasp of its consciousness. Herein lies the origin of the drama of modern civilisation where the consciousness has failed to assimilate most of the realisations of science.

The same retardation had caused the rupture of Ṣiffīn in the Muslim world. The Qur'ân as a philosophical system was a science singularly beyond the horizon of the jâhilî consciousness. This resulted in a reputure between those who had assimilated the new thinking and those who remained attached to their old conceptions and conditions of life that the Qur'ân sought to abolish. This has been the underlying phenomenon of Muslim history for thirteen centuries. Masked by historical trappings, it has nevertheless been periodically surfacing in one crisis or the other, through internecine struggles. The Khârijism and the Mu'tazilism were but—the one on the political and the other on the intellectual plane,—the tentatives to catch up with the Qur'ânic thought that still escaped from a retarding consciousness. In all these conflicts, it was always a question of divorce between the temporal Muslim world and the Qur'ânic thought. If the decadence denoted an imbalance between the temporal Muslim world and the Qur'ânic thought, the renaissance marks the effort of the Muslim consciousness to regain its retardation over the Qur'ânic and modern scientific thought.

The same process could be observed in the history of Europe. The first rupture therein, took place on the moral plane in the name of Reformation, but various schisms as that of Albigenis[1] had already indicated that the Christian consciousness could no longer span the gulf that divided it from a rationalism derived from scientific development. The second, on the political plane, appeared with the French Revolution; it shattered the traditional social structure and replaced it with a statute founded on the equality of individuals. However, this theoretical equality merely established a precarious equilibrium, and one could already discern in the bosom of the third Estate, champion of the new order, a working class tendency among the Jacobins, opposed to a bourgeois tendency. The execution of Robespierre, and the liquidation of the First Commune of Paris resulted in a bourgeoise triumph. However, the conflict remained latent between the two wings of the new society, the bourgeoise who inaugurated the new era of capitalism, and the workers who prepared the advent of a new class: the proletariat.

But the world born out of this double development is full of all the contradictions and ready for all ruptures. In fact, the Third Estate eventually found itself definitely split, when in face of the practical materialism of the European bourgeoisie, the proletariat would set up its "dialectical materialism".

For the moment the conflict was confined on the summit, between the economists of the bourgeois tradition, mainly Adam Smith and Ricardo and the economists of the new school, Engels and Marx—without taking account of the doctrinaire anarchist-syndicalists, like Bakunin. But with the set up of the First International, after the preparatory congresses at Brussels and London, and the Paris Commune in 1871, the disputes between the two opposing forces were carried from the philosophical into the political arena. It was this period in European history marked by a moral, political, and social schism that was contemporaneous with the zenith of the colonial era and the first manifestations of the Muslim renaissance. It was by this double material thrust—bourgeois and proletarian—that the Muslim world became conscious of European influences in its political and intellectual evolution. It was chaos not civilisation that it discovered in this Europe where the ruptures were going to aggravate in terms of the two growingly preponderant factors: the rapidity of scientific development and colonial expansion. These two factors, scientism and colonialism, joined together to become the "fatality" of Europe, just as theology had become that of the post-al-Muwaḥḥid society. Under their influence the slide of Europe into materialism could not but accelerate with the soaring of a prodigiously innovating science. Each invention, each discovery deepened still more the gulf between an overwhelming science and an overwhelmed traditional consciousness.

Drunk with the new forces that it had unleashed, the European "ME" was enticed by its own genius, becoming a slave to the machine that he had created but could not control. Reality became calculable and happiness measurable in quantities of calories and hormones. It was the era of quantity, of "quantitatism" in the consciousnesses. It was also the era of moral relativism, of the commencement of a century that had for its maxim the famous, "all is relative..." One no longer possessed the sense of the "obsolute" since the 20th century positivist like the brain of the machine, no longer understood what went beyond the "relative" perspectives of the matter. The sense of the "absolute" died in the same manner as did the concept of justice, the day it was declared in Europe that a "bad settlement is worth more than a good proceeding", and one dared affirm that "commerce is authorised theft". Thus the quantitatist and relativist Europe killed a good number of moral precepts, stripping them of their title to nobility and transforming them into the pariahs and untouchables of language, banished from usage and from consciousness; and dictionaries became cemeteries of words that no longer made sense since they responded to dead concepts.

In Europe the quantitatism aggravated in terms of the multiplier co-efficient representing technical power on the scale of a tentacular industry that multiplied by tens and hundreds the material appetites of men. It marked the vocation of the child who no longer chose his line for what he could give to society, but for what he could get from it. One sought to obtain a sinecure rather than to satisfy his natural inclination—an excellent preparation for the colonial administrator, who did not even need to maintain the relative "dignity" that prevented him going to the end of his moral relativism at home. On the colonial level, the moral relativist found an excellent pretext in "national sovereignty", and the mask of "dignity" that he managed to preserve at home, melted in the heat of the colonial sun and the passion of unchained appetites: one simply got what one desired.

Within Europe itself one came to acclimatise oneself to the habits, tastes and ideas imported from colonial life. All social articulations became numerical: one produced so much, one paid so much, one bought so much and ate so much; the life revolved solely around "how much". In the technical and mechanical society being edified since 1900, the number reigns supreme and satistics are unquestionable. The human nature, that is, the conscience itself, does not enter into count, since it could not be deciphered or quantified. The human condition becomes a simple numerical function. The machines tick off, calculate, and drag the man to work in their steel meshes. Even human wants are dehumanised and commercialised, and admitted only so far as they are solvent. The general wants of humanity, more particularly those of the "widows and the orphans", the old and the sick are not solvent, and the machines do not make either moral calculation or metaphysical estimates.

The automatism is admirable: the machines turn, the colonies furnish the raw material and cheap labour, the consumers who can pay, consume, the machines calculate the scales, establish dividends, the salaries, the time-table the automatism is admirable.... on condition, of course, that not a single grain of sand entered in the motor.

But there entered more than one in the modern machine. In 1914 there was a sinister grating of brakes. The sources of raw material were not sufficient; there were motors that went idle or did not work to their normal rythm, that is to say, at the scale of an insatiable avidity and voracity. A row broke out amoung the machine owners. After four years of destruction and millions of dead, a precarious *modus vivendi* was established, and the machines started revolving again. In the consciences, drunk with the money and the champagne, the 1914-1918 rupture did not leave any mark, and the apparent prosperity momentarily masked the reality.

However, since 1930 a new grating was audible in the machines. This time the crisis was going to lay bare the moral canker that devoured the civilisation, and to prove that technique could not alone solve the human problems by simple graphs and equations. The machines stopped turning. The queus lengthened before the unemployment pay-offices, and misery installed itself in homes and hearths. A tragic irony presided over this misery, that for the first time in history, issued, not from a scarcity of riches, but from their superabundance. It is the stroke of genius of the 20th century to have transformed scientifically the conditions of welfare into factors of misery. Wherein lay the mischief? In an excess of the curve of production over that of consumption. A child's play for the technician who knew very well to rectify the calculation by simple arithmetic: One must destroy the surplus, and one destroyed wheat, cotton and coffee, while there existed peoples who totally lacked them. And the civilisation that had invented Malthusianism, undertook to refer no longer to the consumers but to the commodities of consumption.

No spiritual authority existed to denounce the scandal. Those who could save Europe from its economic chaos did not have "solvent" wants: the colonised people, who were naked and hungry, and could'nt buy anything because in considering them as mere instruments of work, one has overlooked to take account of them as consumers.

In the, genesis of the phenomenon resulting from the simultaneous impact of scienticism and colonialism, the conflagration of 1939 was only a return of the flame: the moment when Machiavelli turns against himself and Satan destroys his own work. It is the moment when destiny breathes in human veil, which unfolds itself, so that the oracles may be fulfilled. Prophet Muḥammad, had said in fact: "He who digs a well under the feet of his neighbour shall himself fall into it." And fearing more for a nation the injustice that it commits, than the injustice that it suffers, he added: "The power even of the unbelievers shall endure if it is just, but the power of the believers perishes surely, if it is unjust".

The history of our period tragically illustrates these oracles. Europe that should have used its torch of civilisation to guide the march of humanity, employed it to set aflame the colonial world. But it has harvested therefrom, the same chaos, the same disorientation, and the same fatalism before the evil powers of mythology on its own soil, that it has sown in the rest of the world. Because, the Cartesian, learned, industrialised and polished Europe has also its myths, inhibitive in a different manner: while the paralysis of the post-al-Muwaḥḥid society is apathetic and silent, that of Europe is convulsive and hurling². Its myths are infinitely more dangerous since they hold the power of machine and matter, and thus risk to destroy scientifically the countries and the peoples.

In Europe, the mythology is learned and has its academies, doctors and poets. A little before the Ist World War, a young artillers officer, Ernest Psichari, felt himself transported by emotion before the simple but profound faith of the Muslims of Mauritania. It was for him a providential opportunity for introspection and meditation. It matters little if the Road of Damascus leads to a temple, a church or a mosque. Transfigured and converted, Psichari took the path of the church, "the party of my ancestors", as he would note later. Nothing more normal, provided he did not turn the back abruptly on him, who had enlightened his path. In the course of a voyage, in fact, he experienced the urge to vaunt before his young Moorish guide, the material power of modern civilisation. The young beduin replied:

—"You have the earth and we have the heavens."

Psichari should have smiled at such ingenuity. Instead, he wrote in his diary, this significant exclamation:

—"Ah! that is a word that the Muslims must no longer pronounce!"

Whence came this unwarranted cry from a man recently converted? Psichari, the believer, was the nephew of Renan, and his thinking here strangely accorded with that of his uncle (whom he had renounced because of his atheism), who, after the 1871 war wrote the following lines, that express, in another form, the same racism and contempt for humanity:

"... A race of masters and soldiers, that is the European race. Compel this noble race to work in the slaves' prison like the negroes and the Chinese, and it will revolt. Each rebel among us is more or less a soldier who has missed his calling, a being made for heroic life.... Now the life that revolts our workers would render happy a Chinese, a *fellah*, beings not at all martial. Let each do that for which he is made, and all would go well."

Let us overlook the intellectual mediocrity of these lines—the great erudite has more than once thus let his pen wander. One may ascertain, however, that it errs here right into mythology, incidentally betraying the supreme myth that has hierarchically dominated, since the last century, all other myths of Europe.

The uncle and the nephew had received the sacrament from the same fountain: the superiority of the "race of masters", source of the bloody myth, of the monster that has fathered the anti-human colonialism and anti-European Nazism. This myth has demolished the entire Christian moral philosophy and has committed an outrage against God Himself by striving to supplant Him in the European conscience. It resides in the hearts, dwells in the ideas, animates the wills and untiringly inspires the vocations of the young. History of the past century, is a saga of the colonial spirit. The child born in Europe feels himself pre-destined for colonialism. Even if he misses his vocation, he continues, nonetheless to feed his spirit on colonialism, just as he feeds himself on colonial products.

But there is the return of the flame. Colonialism undergoes a transformation in the European consciousness. It engenders a hypernationalism, then moves on, passing through philosophical distillations, refining itself carefully, to become finally the myth of the "chosen race" that would justify the last degree of barbarism. Founded on racial contempt, colonialism engenders a super-racism.

The war of 1914-1918 was in reality only an intermediary term between colonialism and Nazism, a stage in the distillation process. At the time, each invoked for the best of his material interests the propitious entities of modern alchemy: God, the Right, the Man, thus found themselves intermingled with the petrol and the tin. History became an incantation of dead concepts, for recalling them from the hereafter where they had been sent by the civilisation of machine and numbers. This fashion of using religion—as of yore, magic and sorcery— for the safeguard of one's interests is, perhaps, the most monstrous aspect of the Cartesian genius.

But when one invokes God for the performance of fraudulent deeds, for plundering, killing and corrupting, God delegates Satan for perfecting the process and for achieving in the institutions what had commenced in the individual.

The habit of "teaching the native to work", has diverted the coloniser from veritable labour and robbed him of the sense of his civilisation. The practice of injustice has made him forget justice and its fundamentals: respect for law and the sense of the right of the other. The facility of colonial life has made him unaccustomed to all effort, even intellectual, to such a degree that in Algeria the intellectual life of this community which boasts of nearly a million of colonisers, is less intense and less productive than that of a simple town in France.

Thus the coloniser gradually de-civilises, brutalises and degrades himself. He had wished to de-civilise, brutalise and degrade the colonised, but "whosoever digs a pit under the feet of his neighbour.... " The oracle is fulfilled. The coloniser is himself today isolated from his own civilisation whose problems he no longer comprehends. His "anti-indigène" racism has exacerbated his individualism on the national plane and his chauvinism on the global plane.

Thus, little by little, a colonial administration ceases to be an impersonal institution and an organisation of state, and is transformed into a company of individuals or a "gang". It becomes like the old East India Company, "autonomous" in its internal regulations, having almost nothing in common with the interests of the colonising nation and no relationship at all with those of the colonised people. One no longer countenances an administration but coteries of civil servants. Each wants his share and trims for himself the portion that he pretends to be his. It is thus that the *colon* who had abandoned all dignity and moral reserve on the colonial plane is thence brought to abandon all scruple on the national plane.

The oracles are fulfilled....And in its turn, Europe becomes a field wherein the colonial spirit reigns. To recapitulate the slow but sure march of this process, one could not do better than to allow a colonised to speak.

Let us listen for instance to Aimé Cesaire[3] whose very work testifies to the human riches which colonialism must need destroy."One must, first, tell how colonisation works to decivilise the coloniser, to brutalise him in the exact sense of the word, to degrade him, to rouse his latent instincts of lust, violence, racial hatred, moral relativism and show that each time a head is chopped off in Viet-Nam or an eye gouged, and one accepts it in France, a young girl raped, and one accepts it in France, a Malgache executed, and one accepts it in France, there is an acquisition of civilisation that weighs down with its own dead weight, a universal regression that begins to operate, a gangrene that settles in, a source of infection that spreads out, and at the end of all these broken treaties, propagated falsehoods, tolerated punitive expeditions, bound and 'interrogated prisoners', and tortured patriots, at the end of this encouraged racial arrogance, and boastful display, there is instilled a poison in the veins of Europe and the slow but sure drift of the Continent towards savagery...."

"And then one bright day, one is awakened by a formidable return shock: the gestapos bustle about, the prisons overflow, the executioners invent, refine and discuss around easels. One is indignant, surprised. One says: '... Bah! it is Nazism, it will pass', and one waits and hopes and does not admit even to oneself the truth that it is a barbarity, but the supreme barbarity that crowns and resumes all the day to day barbarities; that this comes from Nazism, yes, but before becoming its victim, one has been its accomplice; one has supported this Nazism before being subjected to it, one had absolved it, one had closed one's eyes to it, one had legitimised it, because up to now, it had only been applied to non-European peoples; one had cultivated it; one is responsible for it, and that it wells, it pierces and it drips, before swallowing in its bloody waters all the fissures of the Western, Christian civilisation...."

And the ruptures, the corruptions, the transgressions and betrayals multiply and amplify each day in Europe. By the force of utilising justice as means of repression in the colonies, one has degraded it even in the metropolis. By the force of rigging the elections in the colonies, one has contracted even in Europe the taste for falsification in the civic life. By the force of bullying the consciences of the colonised, one does not respect any conscience whatsoever. One is engaged in constant struggle, vying with each other.

This ruthless struggle is carried on even in the scientific arena. In biology, Lyssenko wished to dethrone Mendel, Wiesman and Morgan. The science, no doubt, gains from such disputes, but, at stake, is not merely a better understanding of the laws of heredity. One fights, more often, for demonstrating that one is stronger. It is not the scientific conscience alone that is torn to pieces, but the conscience of humanity, lending itself to all the ruptures, conflicts and apocalypses. Tragic perspectives open up: a return to the troglodyte age is possible. The atom bomb could inspire, tomorrow, a new urbanism, that of the subterranean era. And in the gigantic mole-holes of monstrous Cartesianopolis, would dwell a human race that has substituted a machine for its brain, numbers for its moral concepts and myths for its God.

Howsoever that may be, the Muslim world can no longer seek guidance in the present chaos from a Western world itself on the verge of apocalypse. For discovering its own sources of inspiration, it must look for new paths. But whatever new paths it might borrow, it could not isolate itself within a world driving towards unity. It is not a question, for it, of breaking with a civilisation that represents a great human experience, but of adjusting relations with it.

TRANSLATOR'S NOTES

1. That is Albigenese—the name given to the adherents of a mass anti-sacramental movement in the south of France in 12th and 13th centuries, that was brutally suppressed on orders of the Church.

2. One finds a remarkable illustration of Bennabi's observation in the contrast between the human samples of the paralysis of the two Societies—The Muslim marabout and the Western hippy.

3. French-speaking nationalist African writer from the West Indies.

●●●

5

THE NEW PATHS

"If the Musulmans repudiate what I say, I predict for them a catastroph similar to that which had engulfed 'Ād and Thamūd; and already the signs thereof are beginning to be felt."

Tantawi Jawhari

5

The post-al-Muwaḥḥid society had created the amoebic being who pushed a Pseudopodium towards an easy prey and digested it quietly. Chance held out to him other preys and thus satisfied his modest needs. The post-al-Muwaḥḥid man had vegetated in this manner for centuries, relying only on Providence to feed him. But colonisation had come, carrying off all that was eatable. The amoebic being no longer had even his mouthful of bread. His stomach,—the amoebic consciousness—was roused and he pushed a pseudopodium towards an imaginary prey which he called "the right". Thus was born the "boulitique", the pseudopodium of a society that was hungry but no longer had anything to satisfy its need of nourishment.

Need is said to be the *first historical act* of the man living in society. Here is an entropic definition that seeks to explain history by a process of consumption—definition that could in Algeria indefinitely prolong the pseudopodium of the amoeba. Moreover; this definition does not respond to the stage of evolution represented by the post-al-Muwaḥḥid society. This society doubtless possessed at least certain rudimentary needs, for example those of eating and drinking. Yet, for the past seven hundred years, it failed to invent even a broom handle. It was certainly not the need that made default. Our grandmothers painfully experienced it when sweeping the floor each morning with the traditional much too short handle that they cursed groaning, because it forced them to stoop and bend in two. Yet the simple idea of adding a handle to their domestic tool never occurred to our unfortunate grandmothers.

For, a need is creative and efficacious only when it is in some sort spiritualised by consciousness that transforms it into an *imperative of action*. The latter alone could permit Muslim society to transform its ideas and needs into *products of civilisation*. On the contrary, since the advent of the post-al-Muwaḥḥid man, the process of production has given way to a simple process of consumption. For making history, it does not suffice a society to have needs but also to possess themes and means of creation.

From this point of view, it will not be without interest to describe evolution in terms of energetics. The law of exchange that governs social life does not, in fact, amount to a simple scheme of equilibrium between production and consumption. Such an equilibrium would be fatal since it would lead to a utilisation of the products without any accumulation of productive forces. Such an equilibrium is, besides, inconceivable and this is what Carnot's principle in thermo-dynamics means: for manifestation of energy there must be a potentialisation, that is to say, an accumulation of energy, causing a fall of potential—like the difference of temperatures in a thermal machine or the voltage in an electrical machine. What had been termed above as "need" must likewise be considered as a fall of potential on the plane of social energies.

In sociology, it is not the need in its immediate form that should be regarded as the first "act" of history but the *initiative* that creates, develops and satisfies it. In other words, there should be a double definition, energetic and entropic. If now, one tries to translate these considerations in the social "category" called politics, one must do so in terms of means rather than needs. Thus, it is neither a question of an exclusive doctrine of 'right' nor an exclusive doctrine of 'duty'. The sociological reality does not call upon the one or the other separately, but simultaneously, linked in a fundamental dialectic that constitutes the mainspring of history. One must not, in any case, overlook the fact that in all ascending development, 'DUTY' must necessarily exceed 'RIGHT'; for there must be an acquirement or in terms of political economy, a 'plus-value'. Judged by this relationship, all politics founded solely on right is nothing but pure demagogy, a pseudopodium that prolongs the amoebic life on the ideological plane,....a "boulitique" in the Algerian sense of the word.

In fact, the duty-right relation is also an ontological relation explaining the genesis of right itself. The latter could not be conceived independently of "duty" which really marks the "first act of history". A politics that does not talk to a people of his duties but only of his rights, is not a politics but a mythology or somber mystification. It is not, besides, a question of teaching words or slogans to a people, but methods and techniques. It is not a question of chanting "liberty" to him; he knows the song. It is not a question of repeating to him that he has "rights"; *he knows it.* There is no need to teach him the virtues of unity; his gregarious nature has already taught them to him. In a word, it is not a question of "revealing" to him what he knows already but of providing him with an efficacious method for the realisation of his capabilities and his knowledge in a concrete social form. To be more exact, it is not a question of talking to him of his rights and of his liberty but of specifying to him means for acquiring them, means that could not but be the expression of his duties. Thus for the post-al-Muwaḥḥid society, it is less a question of demanding the rights than of technically utilising man, soil and time for producing a social synthesis that would automatically engender right by virtue of the indissoluble duality, duty-right.

"To make politics" is to prepare the psychological and material conditions of history,—to prepare the man for creating history. The post-al-Muwaḥḥid individual would make politics when he ceases to be an amoeba waiting for a doubtful prey. He would cease to be a disinherited creature, a prey to all the attacks of colonialism when he would talk a little less of his rights and a little more of his duties; a little less of the Atlantic Charter and a little more of his own resources. He would cease to be an easy prey when he would have rectified his manner of thinking and acting according to a pragmatic logic of action and a Cartesian logic of thought, and when he would have rid himself of the myths that inhibit his activity and limit his efficacy. This condition seems to be gradually realising itself since the Palestine affair which undeniably constitutes the most conspicuous and, in a sense, the most fortunate event of the modern history of the Muslim world.

The Palestinian defeat has inaugurated a new stage in the Muslim renaissance by laying bare all the false values and illusions that had distorted the perspectives of its future. This providential defeat,—this happy victory of the real over the illusory—has liberated spirits and consciences stifled by the chaos. New paths open up, here and now, before a people shaken but awakened, disillusioned but henceforth turned towards the real. The myths could no longer vindicate themselves before the realities hitherto veiled by the halo of sentimental ideologies. The most dangerous psychosis, that of the "easy thing" has suffered a mortal blow. The Muslim consciousness has begun to reflect on the fragility of this Colossus with feet of clay that the Arab league in its ignorance of the reality, had erected against the small state of Israel, offering to the modern world the spectacle of a new episode of the David's fight against Goliath. The Muslim man duped by the lectures on the Rights, the Atlantic Charter and the providential U.N.O; then stunned by the fall of the Goliath, is now recollecting himself which could not but be salutary. A Palestinian intellectual stunned by Israel's all too easy victory has tried to fathom the "profound causes of the chaos". This attempt is worth noting because it is symptomatic of the new state of mind in the Muslim world, a sign of a new turning-point of history.

This is what Doctor Nazem el-Kodsi wrote a few months after the Israeli victory:

> "The profound causes of the Palestine catastrophe are not merely of a military or political character. The defeat has revealed all the social, economic and political shortcomings from which our countries suffer. But it is not enough to know the errors committed and to reveal the defects; it is also essential to draw lessons therefrom and to remedy them. For facing the Zionist danger, it does not suffice to conclude political accords among Arab countries, but first of all one must seek to improve the standard of life, to cleans our social life and re-organise our armed forces. Personally I believe that the social effort must be our principal care. The social life and the life of the classes must be reformed; one could not ask a people to make sacrifices if they are dissatisfied with the form of government. A sick and starving people whose future is not assured, cannot and would not fight for its government. A man cannot exact obedience of his children if he does not provide them a decent life; how could one demand from a people the obedience, the discipline and faith in national ideal, if one does not guarantee him an improvement in his standard of living, proper education and a decent job? We must make haste because in our age rapid development has become an imperative law. I do not intend to under-estimate the importance of political accords or military preparedness, but I believe that a decent life is the essential condition of popular consciousness and faith in the national ideal. Without this consciousness and without this faith, the political and military accords are not worth anything. The Arab League offers us a convincing example. The Arab peoples' indifference towards it, is mainly due to the fact that hitherto it has occupied itself entirely with high politics. Now, an organisation that shows no concern for the life of the individuals from a social and economic point of view cannot retain the interest of the public opinion. The Arab League could still regain its prestige if it applies itself to economic and social problems and works out plans for improving the standard of living. One must liberate the people from economic fear and guarantee their right to education and health. It is the only road

towards a veritable renaissance and the sole means of assuring our existence".*

We have quoted this article at length to highlight the new state of mind in the ruling circles of the Muslim world, and the reservations of the author regarding what he terms the "high politics" and we have named it "boulitique". This new spirit is not confined to the Middle East but seems to pervade the entire Muslim consciousness since the Palestine affair. These words pronounced by a young Moroccan patriot before an U.D. M.A.[1] meeting recently held in Tlemcen express the same anxiety to understand the underlying causes:

"For centuries, one and the same ill has gnawed at the Arab people in the East and the West. It is the lack of confidence in himself, the calumny and the disparagement, the cult of honours, the apology of men. It is this chronic makeshift that has guided the caliphs, emperors and Arab princes to apply to this people the rule of the fist, without any thought for their education and social progress, long before any colonialism had dreamt of exploiting these blemishes as murderous weapons to serve its own ends in the East as well as in the West."

The main point in this somewhat literary criticism is the anxiety to understand the internal evil: the *colonisibility*. These words have an unfamiliar ring in the ears of the Muslim political and intellectual milieu, hitherto solely occupied with the "straw in the eye of one's neighbour". Now, all of a sudden, one becomes aware of the "beam in one's own"! What appears clearly in the article of the Syrian statesman as well as in the simple words of the young Moroccan, is the new notion of "duty" henceforth implicated as an essential political factor. There is a growing consciousness that a lot of efforts must be made in all fields, and duties accomplished, for attaining rights, thus rendered legitimate. This marks the end of the "easy thing",— that what one claimed, one obtained as a "right". One realises at last that the plough cannot be put before the oxen, nor can it be moved merely by superb flights of oratory or flambeaus of patriotic fervour.

Thus the Muslim world turns away from the path of ease it has hitherto followed towards a new path, animated with the will to vanquish rather than elude the difficulties. It also implies the end of another psychosis, that of the "impossible thing". The myth of the impossible begins to disperse, in fact, from the moment one is engaged in the humblest effort. In the social field

* *La Republique Algerienne*, 9 December 1949: "The Standard of Life of the Populations of the Middle East". It would be useful for the readers to reproduce here the brief editorial comment introducing this article: "The defeat inflicted by Israel on the heteroclite coalition of Arab states in Palestine seems to have succeeded in pulling out the peoples of the Middle East from the torpor in which their leaders had plunged them".

each effort has its results and when these results accumulate in a positive balance-sheet of Muslim activities, one would perceive that it is infinitely more effective to accomplish a "duty" than to demand a "right". A new social psychology is taking shape. We could already discern its premises notably in Algeria. The folowing account appears to us significative of the new spirit.

THE SITE OF SAINT-EUGÉNE

"Sunday, 20 November: Rest day on account of the rally organised by the Mosque Committee.

Sunday, 27 November: The weather, at first cloudy, cleared up after 8 A.M; but the volunteers forseeing bad weather did not arrive. However two of them turned up on the site to see the condition of the path after strong rains. It has stood well, needing only a few retouches.

Sunday, 4 December: Three volunteers from Saint-Eugéne and three local inhabitants. Aided by experience, one flounders less. The steps are built of huge stones that would resist all assaults. A slight slope is arranged in each step for allowing the flow of water towards a gutter dug up between the path and the embankment. The path is levelled with the help of a mixture of stones and slaty soil. After a good rain, it forms a compact surface that ensures solidity of the work....

15 meters of the path have been completed.

Observations: Today, during the interval one of the local volunteers offered us tea, creating a cheerful camaraderie. During work we exchange ideas. It is with a certain irony that we return the salam of passers-by. We show due appreciation of their "God help you". We thank them politely but remark to the courteous user of our path that we would also appreciate the aid of his arms. This does not fail to provoke a wide smile, inevitably followed by, 'Today I am busy but next week I would be with you'. It happens that the promise is kept....."*

Here is something quite new. These young Algerians who have built this small road have shown that the site was there, but that it was not a question of lamenting over it but of tackling it resolutely with shovels and pickaxes. But the instruments that have moved the earth have also demolished the psychosis of the "impossible thing". Did they know, these

---

* *La Republique Algérienne*, 16 December 1949.

pioneers, that they had traced the first path in Algerian history that did not pass through the Forum, that is anonymous like those who traced it, and that goes straight in History? It would be better perphaps, if they did not. The pioneers are always obscure. They are content to trace the path of Duty. They could also have talked of their local rights and lamented the fate of the unfortunate Muslim population of Saint-Eugéne. But they preferred to set right the path themselves as unpaid roadsmen* In so doing they have also restored to a fundamental notion its original significance. In fact, the division of work which always accompanies social development, produces the wage-system. But this division masks, as a result, an essential distinction between work and salary. The two notions get confused when work, commercialised, becomes a servitude for the man who is forced to sell his "working hours" to an employer at fixed price. This is quite normal in an organised society where the division of work is operating. But this confusion is prejudicial in a society, still on the way of organising itself because it engenders an inclination to idleness on the part of the individual who finds himself unable to sell his working-hours. The result is translated on the social plane by a moral servitude under the form of the psychosis of the "impossible thing", whereby the individual no longer believes that he could or should work without an employer renumerating his working-hours.

Of course the significance thus restored to work by these young men involves other social conditions. But it is infinitely possible that these conditions would progressively realise themselves as they were formerly realised at the time when the Prophet (S.A.W.) and his companions built the first mosque in Islam. The manifestations surging today, here and there, would, more and more, furnish the canvas of collective activities and multiply further as they join the basic current of renaissance.

This spirit has also entered official preoccupations—yet another consequence of the Palestine affair, as witnessed by the agrarian experiment in Syria. For the first time in modern Muslim world the problem of man and soil had been posed and integrated in a national constitution.** This experience takes into account the man, the nomad, who must be settled and the soil, which must be better adapted to the general condition of a people. The two problems are evidently linked, since one could not settle the nomad without attaching him to the soil. To this end, the Syrian constitution provides for the appropriation of millions of hectares from state land or from big land-owners and

---

* The author finds in this initiative the best illustration of his thesis on the "Half-hour of Duty". See, *Les Conditions de la Renaissance.*

** The Egyptian revolution has just posed these problems in a decisive manner—three years after these lines were written.

its division among the nomads in plots of five hectares each. This agrarian reform, now adopted also by Pakistan, will doubtless transform the entire structure of the Muslim society. It is easy to forsee it from an economic point of view; but in integrating the nomad to the social life, one would, by the same stroke augment the human potential of the country. The very psychological conditions would be transformed by the nomadic ferment. The fresh nomadic nature would also, if one may so express it, fertilise the worn out nature of the Damascene bourgeois. Given the numerical importance of the nomadic element, its assimilation would not take place by a simple and total absorption, a sort of mechanical disappearance, but by a metamorphic diffusion in the Syrian social body. It will also result in an enrichment of the social spectrum of the country where, like all other Arab countries, the differentiations are insufficient and the distinctive characters are little marked.

In all these countries, one ascertains the same lacuna—absence of all variety. There is only the Pasha and the plebien, the intellectual and the illiterate. There is no continuity in the social spectrum, in contrast to Europe where most diverse aptitudes and talents link the fruit of the genius to the work of the hand by a cascade of hierarchical but complimentary values, uniting the labour of the scholar to that of the shepherd, passing by the doctor, the engineer, the architect, the artist, the artisan, the worker and the labourer. This richness of the social gamut is wholly lacking in the present Muslim world. In Algeria, for example, there is at the summit the doctor and almost without transition, the beggar. This social poverty explains the inadequacy of the ruling classes in Muslim countries. For genius is but the eruption of the obscure effort ascending across the entire social stratum of a society, for spouting at its summit. One could see here a real reciprocity between the hand and the thought; where the work of hand ceases, the work of mind is fatally aborted. No longer being able to draw its elements from the depths of the social stratum, genius could no more flower at the summit. That is why the work undertaken in Syria is a work of fecundation, testifying to a ripening of ideas. The dormant energies have been roused and show themselves at the surface of social life, in a national Constitution as well as under the humble roof of a cottage.

So, the Muslim renaissance seems at last determined to emerge from chaos towards order and organisation. This would mark the access of the amoebic man,—a disintegrated and colonisable individual, to a productive life and his reintegration in the framework of a non-colonisible society. On the collective plane, this would imply the transition of the post-al-Muwaḥḥid society to a stage of civilisation characterised by an original synthesis of its own Islamic genius and that of the "modern" genius.

But all this calls for a deep understanding of man, his possibilities and inadequacies, and a serious examination of the social values of Islam. Psychology and sociology are then, necessary for discovering the new values of Muslim renaissance and the new paths still masked by certain post-al-Muwaḥḥid myths. Now, for knowing man, one must first know oneself, and this demands a rigorous introspection on the part of Muslim leaders and a searching examination of conscience. When one wants to find the flaws of a steel bar which is intended to serve as the central motor of a machine, one submits it to an analysis—for example, a mellographical examination, in order to study its internal structure. It will not be reasonable or possible to do otherwise. Similarly when one wishes to know man as the motor of social life, conditions are such on the human plane that one must have recourse to a search of conscience that alone would reveal the intimate articulations of the human personality in its movement and action. Only by this method, one could explore the innermost recesses of the post-al-Muwaḥḥid soul to know where the transformations are needed. In the past, these transformations have always been linked to the "personal experience" of a sort wherein humanity discovers its own reality in the experience of certain men; and religion which is the historical and social expression of these experiences repeated in the course of the centuries, naturally inscribes itself in the origin of all human transformations. We cannot consider humanity solely on the material plane. We know what illusions the projection of any reality on a particular plane can produce,—if in certain conditions a circle would appear a circle, in others it would simply be a straight line. Man is involved in the social life as a psycho-temporal factor. He acts not only in terms of his temporality, of his material needs, but also in terms of his psychism, of his spirituality. Therein lies the complete reality of man which must be taken into account for siezing it in its totality. One could not determine the conditions of his transformation, if any one of the two aspects, moral or temporal, was abstracted. Under the former aspect, he is essentially the *homo religiosus*. Thus the religious notion directly enters in the method of retrospection as the very basis of the conscience in quest of itself. The social, linked to this religious conscience by the man himself, could not be separated from its own moral conscience. Thus, as a point of departure for all social transformation, a religious reform is necessary.

But on what terms the problem would be posed on the particular plane of the modern Muslim world? As we have seen, the Reformist school had posed it in theological terms, while Iqbal posed it in quite other terms, demanding not a science but a consciousness of God, not a theological concept but an "immanence"[2]. The Reformist tendency—which had the merit of breaking the fatal equilibrium of the post-al-Muwaḥḥid period—had directed its appeal mainly to reason, thus restoring the problem to the "intellectual phase" of the civilisation. As a result it burnt up an essential stage of the evolution, the spiritual, that corresponds precisely with the transformation of the individual and the primary transformation of social values.

Thus the return to the "salaf" implied by the doctrine of the classic Reformist movement did not enter the historical order of facts, but constituted a slip that did not bring back the man to the era of early consciousness but to that of the theological science, that is to say, to use again an example of the past, to the post-Ṣiffîn epoch. It thus reduced itself merely to a reform of scholars, that hardly, if at all, touched the human masses. The Algerian case, however, constitutes an exception, thanks to the remarkable personality of Shaykh ben Bâdis whose personal radiation could reach popular consciousness. But, in general, the reformist movement does not seem to retain the spiritual breath, the mystical elan, that had marked its debut. It subsists, as seen, only in the form of an instruction more concerned with the formation of followers than of apostles. It seems besides, that it would be forced to cede place to a tendency more in conformation with the wishes of Iqbal*. In the past fifteen years, associations have sprung up almost everywhere in the Muslim world wherein the Muslim consciousness seeks anew its path. Already before 1939, young Muslims had been meeting in Egypt and Syria under the banner of "Youths of Mohammad".

The most recent movement affirming the new tendency is doubtless that of Muslim Brotherhood in Egypt, which has also numerous followers in Syria. Unfortunately we do not possess enough record on this movement whose essential characteristic as implied in its very title, is the *act of fraternisation*. The first Islamic community was not founded on mere sentiment but on a fundamental act of "fraternisation" between the anṣârs and the muhâjirs. The same pact unites today the modern "Muslim Brothers" in a sort of community of ideas and of goods. The chief of the movement, who is neither a philosopher nor a theologian, is content to revive an Islam stripped of all its historical wrappings. His doctrine is nothing but the Qur'ân itself; yet a Qur'ân with its grip on life. It is true that the classic

* Recent dialogues in the Algerian Iṣlāḥist milieu have shown us, how anxious this milieu is to find a new formula, under the pressure of events and repeated criticism.

Reformists too did not call for any other doctrinal basis. But it may be noted that in the classical school, the Quranic verse is utilised above all as a didactic means in an intellectual training. Quran is thus the supreme authority that furnishes criterea of all sorts—arguments for combating its adversaries and incentives for condemning usages and habits "incompatible with sound Tradition". It even serves as an aesthetic model of literary canon for the usage of an exacting science, the balâgha, or Arab rhetoric.

In any case, the Quranic notion does not directly touch the consciousness and the nature of the post-al-Muwaḥḥid man; it does not touch the source of his life, the vital aspects of his thought and behaviour. It constitutes the means of a "tajdîd" rather than the imperative of "tajaddud". As such, however, its social significance remains doubtless considerable and it must be assigned a place at the basis of the present renaissance. "Tajdîd" furnishes the psychological explanation of what we have termed the "accumulation". At the same time it constitutes a sort of material condition or rather material bait, to "tajaddud", renewal of self, which forms the very essence of renaissance, while "tajdîd"—renewal of spirit—is but the appearance thereof.

With the movement of Muslim Brothers, it is primarily the Quranic value that renews itself, becoming essentially an active value and a technical means of transforming the man. Muslim scholars who have had the occasion to approach Ḥasan al-Bannâ affirm that by his intermediation, the Quranic verse becomes a living imperative, dictating to the individual a new deportment and drawing him irresistably to action. The Quranic notion acts as if it was suddenly renewed on the lips of the head of "Muslim brothers". On reading that it is "renewed", some would be shocked in so far as this "renewal" might be linked in their minds to a "sorcery" on the part of al-Bannâ.

However, there is nothing mysterious about it. This secondary school teacher who goes to say his Friday prayers alternately in the various mosques of Cairo, takes advantage of these occasions by recalling to the faithful certain precepts of the Qur'ân. He does not offer any exposition which he leaves to the al-Azhar teachers, more learned than him in the subject. Besides, the field of exegesis is that of philological, theological, philosophical, juridical and, indeed, historical exploration; it is the sphere of science. The expositor could only say what may be true, and in which he himself and all his listeners believe. But this verity is related to reality on the intellectual plane only--a purely theoretical relation with science. Even supposing that what the expositor says may not occasionally be debatable as an abstract notion, it could never be the catalyser of a radical transformation of fundamental sociological factors in a social synthesis.

Yet, it is only such a catalysis that could establish an organic relationship between a social doctrine and its object. In this field one may compare the teachings of the classical Reformist school and the movement of "Muslim brothers". On the one side, "Islamic solidarity" is founded on the notion of "fraternity" which is only a sentiment; while with Ḥasan al-Bannâ the same notion becomes "fraternisation"—fundamental act by which one makes himself a "Muslim Brother". This act, so simple, is in reality a total transformation of man who passes from the post-al-Muwaḥḥid stage to that of renaissance, just as he had once passed from the jâhilian society to the Islamic community. For operating this transformation of the individual, the leader of the "Muslim Brothers" makes use only of the Quranic verse but he uses it in the same psychological conditions wherein it was used formerly by the Prophet (S.A.W.) and his companions. Here lies the entire mystery—to utilise the verse not as a written notion but as a notion revealed.

If Hasan al-Bannâ overwhelms his audiance, it is precisely because he does not interpret Quran but *reveals* it to the consciousness that he overwhelms. On his lips the Qur'ân is no longer a cold document, a written word, but the gushing forth of a living verb, a light that comes directly from heavens, that illuminates and guides, a source of energy that galvanises the wills. It is not the theological and rational God that he manifests, but the acting, immanent God whose breath the Muslims physically felt at Badr and at Ḥunayn, the Quranic verity, here, directly verifies itself by its direct effect on the consciousness and by its action on men and things. The "notion", more or less abstract, cedes place to a "value" concrete and present—an active synthesis of thought and action that reciprocally blend with each other in a society that thinks of its action and acts on its thought.

The teaching of al-Bannâ is a personal experience that draws its inspiration not from a document, the letter of the Qur'ân but from the very source of its revelation; the fruit of this experience can be seen in the form of an "acting truth" in all fields of life. It changes the psychology of the individual at the very basis of life. The young Egyptian who used to spend his patriotism in blazes of oratory demanding his rights, understands that the only path of achieving them is that of duty and ascertains his possibilities, his power over persons and things, from the moment he embarks on this path. He becomes the apostle whose appeal touches, transforms and guides other men, who in their turn become new Brothers. A gigantic machine is set in motion that moves the entire life of the country,—creating banks for directing capital, a powerful press for orienting culture, an industry for creating and orienting work. Millions are collected and invested by the "Muslim Brothers" who have thus established the two necessary bases of individual life, moral and material. Despite the dissolution of the "Muslim Brothers" and the execution of its chief, it is most probable that the germs sown by the latter would achieve their harvest. The ideas identified with the permanent elements of human consciousness, cannot disappear. They keep pace, often obscurely, with the current of this consciousness, surfacing, metamorphosed, at a historic moment. Just as the ideas of Ibn Taymiya have surged in modern Islam in the form of *Iṣlâḥ*, those of al-Bannâ could not henceforth be separated from the evolution of the Muslim world, wherein they have renewed the "moral tension" and opened, perhaps, the most fruitful path*. That is why we have not adhered to the chronological order in talking of this experience that we consider more in the light of a land-mark than an end. This experience belongs to the Muslim world as one of the perspectives for escaping from its present chaos and would be inscribed in modern Muslim history as the first positive tentative of a bio-historical synthesis. It would polarise the ideas of the present Muslim world, incorporating in its evolution the modern technical element. It would also establish a bridge spanning history, beyond the deviation of Ṣiffîn to the very source of the Muslim soul, over and above the paralyses, the mythologies and equivocations of the post-al-Muwaḥḥid society. It represents the first effort of the reconstruction of Muslim society, referring to the plan of its first architect—Muḥammad.

The social synthesis has begun to operate even if in an anarchical fashion. This anarchy would disappear once the technical spirit that has become a factor of acceleration of history, would assume direction of the present evolution.

---

* The various considerations recorded above remain valid as far as the personal experience of the founder, Ḥasan al-Bannâ, is concerned. However, following a very recent visit to the East, the author feels obliged to modify his judgement on the movement itself. The latter, under the direction of its new leaders, seems to have become rather a political instrument, despoiled of the civilising character that one would have, above all, wished to see therein. In its new phase, the movement even appears to utilise religion merely for achieving certain immediate practical ends. (1954).

TRANSLATOR'S NOTES

1. L'Union démocratique du manifeste algérian, the moderate Algerian Political party headed by Ferhat Abbas.

It is remarkable how Bennabi grasps Iqbal's concept of religion from Gibbs' scanty reference. According to Iqbal, religious life in its final phase that betokens a shift from metaphysics to psychology "develops an ambition to come into direct contact with the ultimate Reality. It is here that religion becomes a matter of personal assimilation of life and power, and the individual achieves a free personality, not by releasing himself from the fetters of law, but by discovering its ultimate source within the depth of his own consciousness. As a Muslim Sufi put it, 'no understanding of the Holy Book is possible until it is actually revealed to the believer as it was revealed to the Prophet'. Iqbal's views on the subject led Gibb to remark that the theology that Iqbal attempts to re-instate is not, in fact, the orthodox theology but the Sufi theology. (Gibb, H.A.R. *Modern Trends in Islam* Chicago: University of Chicago Press, 1947, p. 82).
Iqbal, however, deplores that religion in the sense he understood it, goes under the unfortunate name of mysticism supposed to be a life-denying, fact-avoiding attitude of mind, directly opposed to the radically empirical outlook of modern times. (Iqbal, *Reconstruction of Religious Thought in Islam,* Lahore: Sheikh Ashraf, 1930. Reprinted 1944. pp. 197 and pp. 180-181).

6

MUSLIM WORLD: A PREAMBLE

6

The Muslim world is no isolated social group that could achieve its evolution in a closed vase. Its double participation as actor and witness in the human drama demands an adjustment of its material and spiritual existence to the destinies of humanity. For integrating itself efficaciously in the world evolution, it must know the world, know itself, make itself known and proceed to an evaluation of its own values as well as all the values that constitute human patrimony. It is, doubtless, a difficult task in a world whose evolution does not obey any criteria. Noting these fact Gibb remarks in his usually exaggerated manner that

> "... Instead of a broad current of soundly based and rationally acceptable arguments, modernism, lacking the discipline of controlled thinking often loses itself in a maze of subjective impulses and is ever liable to the danger of plunging headlong over some unseen precipice".[1]

However, as we have noted in the preceding chapter, this empiricism seems to be replaced, since the Palestine affair, by a critical spirit and a care for method; and the judgements and actions of the governments seem more and more oriented towards a better understanding of itself and the other, and by a deeper appreciation of the West and its spirit, even if it has not yet resulted in concrete social action, extending to the entire Muslim world, and in a consciousness of its resources. The Muslim world has not still arrived at technical action which alone could accord it a place in the modern world where a sense of efficacy stands first in the scale of values. This necessity has become all the more imperative for the world stands today at the end of a term that has lasted for centuries and the commencement of another, marked from the very outset by the Shakespearien dilemma: To be or not to be.

In fact, the present conditions are so contradictory that the chances of humanity seem to be equally divided between the one or the other alternative. If scientific and economic factors have put the world in a state of prefederalism, the ideas on the contrary, have maintained, therein, all the ferment of discord and conflict. One finds again here, at its most violent, the imbalance that has always existed between a retarded consciousness and a progressive science. Only this time the imbalance has become incompatible with the very existence of the species. The economic conditions created by the 19th century have gradually imposed, in various fields, positive measures that have given the world a planetary character. The birth of international organisations, social, economic and political, bears witness to the growing necessity felt by people all over the world, to organise their lives in common. Thus every day one sees the outline of a universal federation asserting itself. This tendency has become even more pronounced since the last War and today assumes many new aspects, not the least picturesque among them is that illustrated by the "citizen of the world".

It is most of all the technical factor that has accelerated this movement. Technique has abolished space, leaving only the distance of their culture among the peoples. But the latter seems only to have increased, when one thinks of the poor wretch in Algeria where none bothers to educate him, and the man who disintegrates the atom in U.S or Russia. Science has abolished the geographical distances between men but an abyss persists between their consciousness. Thus the facts and the ideas contradict each other. The world has become a tiny, extremely inflammable ball wherein the fire that touches one end could instantly spread to the other. It is no longer possible to divide the problems and the solutions, to treat Europeanism in separation from colonialism. Only twenty years before, the Indo-Chinese conflict would have been confined to its geographical borders. Today, it is as much the concern of a docker from Oran—interested as a colonised—, as that of a Japanese, interested as a consumer of rice. The world has been shaken from top to bottom. A new page commences in history under the heading: Humanity must be one or cease to exist.

Would the world leaders find a happy and peaceful solution to this dilemma? Unfortunately, if one could judge from their actions, they give the desultory impression of somnambulant painters busy in repainting an old worm-eaten building while pick-axes attack its foundations to pull it down. The painting brush is a ridiculous and out of the place instrument on a ruined site where one needs shovels and trovels for clearing the debris of the old world and for building the new. But if men would refuse to build the new world, it would come into being itself, in its own manner. Certain ideas still maintain colonialism, but the factors of its annulment would, in the end, prove decisive. But for the moment this contradiction is tragic. One might well wonder, what could the proclamations of the "respect for the human person" and the "declaration of human rights" signify to men, domesticated, nativised and "civilised" in the colonialist manner? At the basis of all this we find the common denominator,—a materialist culture that could promote an empire or imperialism but not a civilisation.

Endowed with all the inertia of the matter, this culture is incapable of following the evolution of its own products. It has immured itself in this even by its own Cartesian method. One is pre-occupied not with finality but with causality. The problem of the destination of the object with regard to man has yet to be posed to the Western conscience—one produces, but is incapable of distribution. The rationalist Europe that has created the machine, finds itself incapable of posing the human problems. All non-measurable relationships escape his consciousness. One knows how to fashion the matter but does not know how to render it useful to man. The process of production in Europe does not define the object by its relation to man, but defines the utility of man with regard to the fabricated object.

Europe has become technician but has ceased to be moral, no longer able to discover human perspectives beyond the numbers, the quantity, beyond the limits of a world solely defined in material terms. A civilisation finds its equilibrium between the spiritual and the quantitative, between finality and causality. As soon as this equilibrium breaks down in one direction or the other, there comes the vertical fall. The Muslim civilisation lost its equilibrium the moment it ceased to observe the just relation between science and conscience, between the material factors and the spiritual order, thus, foundering in pure metaphysical anarchy and maraboutic chaos that have formed its decadence. We are witnessing today, another disequilibrium—the Western civilisation that has lost the sense of the spiritual, finds itself, in its turn, at the brink of the abyss.

Thus for the Muslim world, it is no longer a question of separating values but of coupling science and conscience, ethics and technique, physics and metaphysics, in order to realise a world according to the law of its causes and the imperative of its ends. But for reviving its vigour to the world, their must be a new man capable of assuming the responsibilities of his existence, morally and materially, both as a witness and an actor. The post-al-Muwaḥḥid man is certainly too old, too decrepit; but the Muslim world, nonetheless, contains a large share of this necessary youthfulness. The Muslim has retained, in fact, despite his colonisibility an essential sense of the moral value which the old modern spirit lacks. At the same time, Islam is on the way to renew itself, thanks to the Cartesian value.

This synthesis which is slowly taking place, would no doubt gain momentum once problems begin to be tackled with the scientific spirit that has become the factor of the acceleration of history. This method singularly shortens the stages and eliminates those unnecessary. The medieval, traditional Japan that opened its doors to Commodore Perry in 1868, cleared in one stage the distance that separated it from the 20th century. But it has done so technically, methodically, by tightening its schedule and scientifically utilising man, soil and time. The Muslim world must, in its turn, jump over the interval of its retardation by tailoring its means and activities. The Palestine affair has brought home to it the necessity of such a course while indicating certain new paths. It now seems willing to commence a new experience, taking into account the drawbacks and errors of the past, without which the lesson of history, more particularly of the last years, would lose all significance. Certain stages, like nationalism, which once appeared necessary are no more than archaism bypassed by history.

The present world is a product of the inevitable disintegration of the colonist and colonisable world that we knew ten years ago. But, at the same time, this disintegration has laid bare the profound sense of history; on the one hand, it has revealed the unity of problems and needs in the world, and on the other, highlighted the necessity of re-adjusting relations among peoples. Colonialism and nationalism are alike condemned. Colonialism is no longer compatible with an international existence which could not be based on force; the universal conscience would solemnly condemn it as the cause of troubles, regression and war. Hitherto the colonial compact could attack the life, consciousness and even the very existence of the colonised and one turned a blind eye in the "civilised" countries. Now international diplomacy finds itself faced with a dilemma: the colonial compact or the human compact. One could not form part of a human order when one is either colonised or coloniser.

The world is well on the way to realise itself on a planetary scale, to totalise itself, its resources and its needs. It is in a fair way to realise institutionally the direction of history. "Liberalism" cedes place to a rational order that tends towards general harmony, not in accordance with vague Utopian plans, but with strict law of vital necessities. The Muslim world would have to take into account this decisive step of history in its own evolution. Formulas such as pan-Arabism and pan-Islamism are, henceforth, just as obsolete as pan-Europeanism that one wants to resurrect at Strasbourg.

Of course, optimism and pessimism are alike forbidden as regards the chances of peace. But it must be stated that countries do not seem to understand the significance of the decisive stage which the World is about to clear as expressed by the title of the work "The World is One". Still its author seems concerned only with the spatial aspect of this unity that cannot but strike a person crossing the 360 degrees of the globe in a few hours. But the unity of the world has always been the essential phenomenon of history while the divisions constitute mere accidents, the epi-phenomena. If it escapes the Cartesian mind, it is because its formative culture ascribes the commencement of history to the foundation of Rome, and of thought to the academies of Athens. It is curious how, even the greatest European minds seem incapable of rising above the hellenic thought. As soon as they cross the frontier of "Greco-Latin humanities", they seem to be wandering on another planet. One must, all the same, note a new tendency evident in the work of a Guenon or a Huxley, systematically studying and bringing to light the common foundations of mystical thought in the world.* These efforts are doubtless still fragmentary and too recent. Moreover they only touch reality at the top; therefore, it is as yet hard to determine their effects on the daily relations and direct contacts between men and peoples. However, converging with the facts already mentioned, they provoke humanity to resolve its dilemma.

In any case, the Muslim world is already, by its very atavism, half-way towards the new world. However backward, the Post-al-Muwaḥḥid man realises better than the civilised man the psychological conditions of the new man, the "citizen of the world", or according to the prophetic expression of Dostoievski, of the "Omni-man". To be sure, he must still attain the material level of the present civilisation by applying all his faculties of adaptation to the temporal order of the atomic era, so deeply marked by the technical spirit. But his role remains, above all, spiritual, as moderator of the excesses of materialist thought and national egoisms. Already, while tracing the path of its spiritual renaissance, Iqbal had called for the Muslim world a turn of mind capable of considering things and institutions "not from the standpoint of social advantages or disadvantages to this or that country, but from the point of view of the larger purpose which is being worked out in the life of mankind as a whole ....".[2] This metaphysics of Iqbal could undoubtedly shock minds warped by a rationalism to which all that escapes the known dimensions seems irrational; but the question is worth posing since it governs the attitude of the man in the new world and the future of civilisation.

---

* Aldous Huxley, *La Philosophie Eternelle.*

It would be proper, here, to adopt the cosmic point of view for seizing the integral sense of history. The eminent Swiss historian, Gustave Jecquier, after studying a four thousand years' slice of Egyptian history, arrived at certain significant conclusions:

> "We ascertain" he says, "that among this people, the civilisation, once its path had been traced, follows it without ever straying from it. Even political upheavals failed to force it out of the path climbing in gentle ascent. The great historical crises, however, permit us to mark a certain number of stages in the history of civilisation and by grouping them in periods, to discern better the progress realised in the course of centuries...."*

Here is a view that envisaging quite a large perspective of history, seems to embrace two distinct orders of facts: On the one hand, a civilisation that follows "a path mounting in gentle ascent", and on the other "the political upheavals" with all the inherent human contingencies—the triumphs, the fanfares, the births, the funerals and the sorrows.

On the one hand, a harmonious line traversing without a break the millenaries, and on the other, the human drama with its upheavals. But this clearly marked distinction between the two orders does not break their unity. The link between the two is of a dialectical nature: man is the fundamental condition of all civilisation and civilisation constantly fixes the *human condition*. Seized in their total human perspective, even the most ordinary facts acquire a significant complexity. For example, in a town a wedding is a commonplace event; evidently, it has a meaning for the married couple and their families, but it also matters to the simple beggar, since the Muslim tradition offers him on this occasion a meal that would sustain for a day his precarious existence. Thus the same event could concern different lives and link up different orders of facts. These liasions are sometimes very subtle; a man could die in Algeria because another man has done or not done such and such a thing that day in Sidney. This remark becomes all the more true when an event gets more complex and goes beyond the individual, local or even national plane. Certain events surpass the framework of simple, rational interpretation founded on immediate human factors, material, moral or political and appear rather to partake of an irrational order whose content could not be seized by Cartesian reasoning.

* Gustave Jecquier, *Histoire de la Civilisaion egyptienne.*

Among the many such examples furnished by history is that of Tamerlane, whose epic clearly extends the historical perspective beyond that of simple human design. For a "rational" construction of the history of this epic, one would, of course, re-assemble its elements and co-ordinate them in accordance with the central figure of its hero. One would perceive, however, that the rational elements pertaining to the man and his personal factors do not give us a satisfactory explanation of his career. In fact, this man was no mercenary or a simple bearer of sword. His religious and political sense, his military and administrative genius make him a complex but perfectly defined personage. Yet we find him wielding his sword against the Golden Horde[3] that was in a fair way to conquer Europe, under the energetic direction of Toghtamich. We see equally the redoubtable blade of Tamerlane descending, neither on China, the legacy of his ancestor, Chengis Khan, nor on India, the future conquest of his descendant, Babur, but on the Ottomon empire where Bazajet[4] had assembled an army of five hundred thousand men for conquering Vienna. Why this singular behaviour? The dynastic right, ambition, the unique chance of an easy victory, religious sentiment, that is to say, all the human factors of policy and military strategy were on the same scale of the balance. Why then do we find the other scale inclining? The Golden Horde as well as the army of Bazajet, is destroyed. One has right to demand what imponderables could have acted here to tilt thus the balance of history? Such a question may be regarded as surprising under the pretext that it belongs to the metaphysical order.* But for giving to the events an integral interpretation compatible with all their contents, one must envisage them, not only in relation to the causality but of their finality in history. Under this relation, it might be necessary at times to reverse the historical method—to see the phenomena in perspective instead of seeing them in retrospective, to consider them in their culmination rather than in their point of departure. For understanding the epic of Tamerlane, for example, one must ask what would have happened if Toghtamish had occupied Moscow and then Warsaw and if

* In his imposing work, *L'Histoire*, which is under publication, Arnold J. Toynbee appears to have considered this question, as is evident from extracts of this work that appeared in French translation in 1953 under the title *Guerre et civilisation*, (Gallimard, ed.). The English author does, in fact, affirm (p. 147) "the blindness of Tamerlane" that he sees culminating in the destruction of what he calls—using the terminology of Oswald Spengler—the "Iranian civilisation". But he does not seem to have noted,—having taken a stand solely from the point of view of autodestructive militarism—the capital importance of this "blindness" of the Tatar emperor for the ulterior course of general history. Because it was well the sword of Tamerlane that cleared a path for the nascent Western civilisation amidst the perils of the sunset descending on the Muslim world.... Could one, in these circumstances, talk of a "blindness", or must not one rather see therein, the manifestation of a supreme *lucidity* beyond the simple intelligence of Tamerlane? (1954).

Bazajet had planted his standard on the monuments of Vienna and thereafter of Berlin? In such a case Europe would have inevitably passed under the triumphant sceptre of Islam. But then, does not one see quite another perspective surging out of history? One sees the renaissance of Europe—still in gestation—melting into the "Timourid renaissance". But while equally brilliant, the two did not have the same significance. The one was the dawn that shone on the genius of Galileo and Descartes, the other was but the beautiful twilight that had already enveloped the Muslim civilisation in its decline. The one was the commencement of a new order, the other, the end of an order drawing to its close. Nothing then, could have saved the entire world from the night that was softly stealing over the Muslim countries. Had Tamerlane but followed his own impulse, nothing could have stopped the end of civilisation.

Howsoever that may be, the tenor of historical facts is not so simple as might appear from a merely individual or national point of view. There is according to Iqbal a "plan d'ensemble" that reveals the direction of the events. Why did Tamerlane prevent Bazajet and Toghtamich from planting Islam in the heart of Europe? So that Christian Europe may pursue the civilising effort which the Muslim world, at the end of its last breath since the 14th century, was no longer capable of doing. The epic of the Tatar Emperor illuminates a finality of history since it has had a conclusion conforming to the continuity and perenniality of civilisation; so that its cycles may succeed each other, and the perpetual relay of genius may continue to operate on the path of progress. A cycle born in certain psycho-temporal conditions develops therefrom, and when the human civilisation has outstripped them, it is the end of a cycle. Another commences in new conditions that would, in their turn, be passed by. It is this law that traces across the millenium of history, this "path mounting in gentle ascent" that humanity slowly scales. The finality of history mingles with that of man.

TRANSLATOR'S NOTES

1. Gibb, *Modern Trends in Islam*, (Chicago, 1947), p. 49. (French translation by B. Vernier. Paris: G.P. Maisonneuve, 1949. p. 82).

2. Quoted from Gibb, p. 101. Also Iqbal, *Reconstruction of Religious Thought in Islam*, (Lahore, 1944), p. 167.

3. Name given to a body of Tartars who invaded Europe in the 13th century and led by Batu, a grandson of Jenghis Khan, crossed Russia into Hungary. They were finally halted and defeated by Taimur-i-Lang about 1395.

4. I.e. Sultan Bayazid, defeated by Tîmur-i-Lang at Angora in 1402.

CONCLUSION

THE SPIRITUAL DEVELOPMENT OF ISLAM

At the end of this study, it is clearly apparent to me that it lacks a second part that would clarify certain aspects that I had to leave aside on the way because of concern for method. Here, I can only indicate these aspects, leaving to someone else the care of treating them properly.

During long centuries Islam has remained static, as if congealed in the forms we have described, and which engendering colonisibility in the post-al-Muwaḥḥid society, have resulted in colonisation. Today Islam is again on the move and commands a future. In other words, its history has become re-animated and begins to live again, starting from a situation in motion and in line with certain horizons recently glimpsed. The concept of vocation covers these two aspects: the conditions of a movement and its finalisation by the human collectivity in these conditions.

Could one talk in this double sense of a vocation of Islam? To say the truth, it does not seem that the Muslim world is still clearly conscious of its spiritual destiny. So far only the Movement of "Muslim Brothers" seems to have made any serious effort to respond to a vocation. But whatever may still be the state of the chaos in the Muslim world today, one could already discern two tendencies that are not of the same nature. The one is of the historical order and is imputable to certain internal forces that manifest themselves as actions and reaction of colonisibility and colonisation; we have studied their constituents—Reformism and Modernism—that impart to Islam its present physiognomy. The other—even if it is not possible to disassociate it from the historical evolution—presents itself, nevertheless, under quite a different form and stems, this time, from the great phenomena of the transfer of civilisation on a planetary scale: it relates to the transfer of the centre of Islamic gravity from the Mediterranean to Asia.

Indeed, one must regard the end of the Mediterranean era as one of the essential phenomena of the last fifty years.

The world centred on the Mediterranean has ceased to exist. Under the shock of the two World Wars, it has been replaced by a world in the form of an ellipse that henceforth draws its inspirations from two distinct focuses. The Muslim world, doubly polarised, now seems besides, to yield to the attraction of Djakarta rather than of Cairo or Damascus. This transfer to an Asian phase implies for it pychological, cultural, moral, social and political consequences that would govern its present as well as its future, primarily in the formation of a *collective will.*[1] Hitherto this will has remained confused and in a diffused state amidst a complex of habits, traditions and prejudices, varying according to space and time, expressing itself sometimes through a heteroclite nobility without popular roots sometimes through a scholarship devoid of horizons. Thus the Mediterranean Islam was dynastic through the *pasha* and his feudal overlords, tribal and nomadic at the level of the Arab-Berber *emir,* dogmatic and imprisoned in the closed vase of its decomposition under the authority of the *Shaykh.* Fully conscious of the benefit it could derive from them, colonialism did its best to re-inforce the influence of this nobility and sham elite with a view to maintain the colonisibility by maintaining the status quo.

The end of the Mediterranean era marks for Islam its liberation from internal shackles. This is particularly visible in Pakistan, as well in Java—countries of relatively recent Islamic acclimatisation, that is to say, new and young countries where thought and action must need surpass the tradition of a closed science, and where Islam is called upon to renovate and activate itself and to learn again to live. The structure of its new social climate is, in fact, not hierarchical but broadly popular. On the other hand, it must adapt itself, therein, to the genius of agrarian peoples and their innate sense of work—thence the promise of a new synthesis of man, soil and time, and consequently of a new civilisation. Finally, it would be obliged to adapt itself to a new spiritual climate in the neighbourhood of this complex India where the thought of Vedas still radiates.

One can well imagine what could become the collective will of an Islam, rid of its post-al-Muwaḥḥid gangue, thus planted in the soil, guided by an elite for whom the Quranic thought, ceasing to be a precious archeological document, classified, filed and closed, would appear as a perpetual evolution. One should not, also, underestimate the role which contact with Indian mysticism could play in this regard.

In its Mediterranean era, if the neighbourhood of Islam with Christian thought has not enriched it spiritually, it did not force it either to transform itself. The contact between two religious thoughts took place, in fact, in the colonial context thus gravely distorting Christian thought in the eyes of the Muslim who could easily feel himself superior to such and such rapacious colonist, presumably Christian but installed in injustice and exploitation. Thus he suffered no inferiority complex on this plane, that is to say, no provocation to recapture and re-think his faith. It seems that the moral apathy of the Mediterranean peoples is attributable, to a large extent, to this sort of complascent pride and selfsufficiency concerning their religion that they implicitly assume vis-a vis a colonialist brand of Christianity.

The contact of the Asiatic Muslim elite with other religions took place in quite other conditions. Here, Islam could not but feel a sentiment of being on foreign soil. At the same time a conqueror and a minority, it lives on a soil already occupied by other religions. India is the land of Brahmanism and Budhism. Here a Muslim community of ninety million finds itself submerged in a mass of three hundred million Hindus; and the Muslim daily witnesses there the extraordinary life of these beings who are undoubtedly among the most religious of the world, and who live in an atmosphere aflame with mysticism. Therein lies for him the source of a profound revolution. It is before this spectacle and in this atmosphere that has ripened the consciousness of an Iqbal, that has acquired, in this great thinker and poet, the rich subjectivity of a consciousness endowed at the same time, with reason and affectivity, with the faculty to understand and to vibrate. This dialogue between the heart and thought which the post-al-Muwaḥḥid man lacked and which still does not seem to have revived in him on the Mediterranean littoral, is not the least lesson that Islam could draw from its transfer towards the Asian sphere.

The Muslims of Java and of Pakistan present, however two distinct characters. The Dutch occupation stretching over many centuries has not left in the Sunda Islands, much intellectual equipment. But the meagre elite forced to wage a struggle against collective pauperism, almost total illiteracy, corruption in all the ranks of administration and lastly, against negligence and the anarchy, deliberately created by a colonialism that has finally taken refuge in the maquis, already shows the marvellous disposition implicit in the genius of the Indonesian people. The man from Java is minute; he has the sense of order and organisation, the love for detail. He is a man, solid, positive and capable of exertion—a practical and technical man who, at the same time, is also a man of arts.

In Pakistan, the British left a certain intellectual hard core of undeniable quality. Syed Amir Ali, the first modern apologist of Islam and Sir Mohammad Iqbal, its first thinker (this old student of Oxford[2] like his *alter ego*, Rabindranath Tagore) belong to this notable elite.

Such appears the new path that lies before Islam, but of course, with one reservation: One must also take into account the international conjunctures which could offer very variable and often unexpected conditions for the realisation of the perspectives that we have underlined, not to speak of the hypothesis of a world war, whereby all the known aspects of human existence would risk being, at the least, transformed.

TRANSLATOR'S NOTES

1. Bennabi seems to echo Iqbal's words in the course of his historic 1930 Address, when demanding the formation of a consolidated Muslim state in the best interest of India and Islam, he observed that it would mean "for Islam an opportunity to rid itself of the stamp that Arab imperialism was forced to give it.... " For a discussion on the singular affinity of mind between the two great thinkers, see Asma Rashid, "Iqbal and Malek Bennabi" *Iqbal Centenary Papers*, Vol. II, (Lahore: University of the Punjab, 1977).

2. Actually Iqbal got admission in Cambridge, before taking his Ph.D. degree from Munich in Germany.

INDEX

●●●